Unseen Liability

The Irreversible Collision of Technology, Risk, and Everything Else.

by Drew Bartkiewicz

Unseen Liability

This book, *Unseen Liability*, was originally written in 2010 with predictions that have now come to pass.

It is now re-released in 2018, in its original version, as the emergence of widespread *Information Malpractice* sweeps across business, politics, media and culture on virtually every continent of the planet.

Unseen Liability

Unseen Liability is a tribute to any person who strives to make the Internet a sustainable place for civic progress, secure global commerce, and the elevation of humanity.

Dedicated to my loving wife, children, and parents. In memory of my late grandmother, Marion Bleakley, a woman who invited people to an upright posture, of seeking to understand more than to be understood.

- *Drew Bartkiewicz*

Unseen Liability

Table of Contents

Foreword

Introduction

Chapter 1: A Data Explosion

Chapter 2: A Communications Revolution

Chapter 3: The Emergence of Technology Blind Spots

Chapter 4: The Birth of Information Malpractice

Chapter 5: The Other Side of New Media

Chapter 6: Respecting the Internet Environment

Chapter 7: CIO Insurance—Hedging against Uncertainty

Chapter 8: Information Malpractice in Every Industry

Chapter 9: Advertising 2.0—Building Our Own Mousetrap

Chapter 10: The Organizational Impact of Technology Risk

Epilogue: Our Lives within the Clouds

Foreword

The last fifteen years of the Internet's existence have been described as disruptive, innovative, unpredictable, and, yes, very uncertain. Few individuals I know have had the benefit of living with and assessing the true impact of this major technological and economic shift in our nation…and our world. Whether or not the business world fully appreciates the new reality, business risk, reputation and economic success now run through servers, databases, and computers. All connected – for better or worse - through the World Wide Web. *Unseen Liability*, with its stunning recognition and invention of the term "information malpractice," offers the reader a truly original and understandable baseline from which to judge not only our progress with technology, but to predict the emergence of technology blind spots in virtually any industry. By relying on his experiences in both the technology sector and the financial services industry, Mr. Bartkiewicz makes the convincing and clearly original argument that the gap between what business (and people) *can* do with technology is rapidly outpacing what they *should* do. In fact, he boldly, and accurately, suggests that traditional economic and risk evaluation models were written for a world that no longer exists.

Unseen Liability

Every week the media reports an unexpected business interruption, a major data breach, or a public Internet disaster, yet until now no one person has connected the dots of our world's technology dependence to start to define where human error ends and technology error begins. Through real-world examples demonstrating technology arrogance as well as technology ignorance, *Unseen Liability* suggests that the speed and breadth of technology advancement has outpaced the CEO's ability to predict risk – and their future.

This book is not about insurance; quite the contrary. I believe *Unseen Liability* is the new lens through which all business leaders should view their role in balancing risk and reward in the information age. Technology mastery has become both an economic accelerant and the dominant risk for business leaders. Relying upon his exceptionally diverse, international business experience, as well as his interaction with the World Economic Forum, Yale University, the Brookings Institution, and others, Mr. Bartkiewicz leads us through the logical argument that perhaps the cost to *use* technology has been replaced only by the much larger cost to *fail* with technology.

As the Internet environment rapidly evolves from supporting basic e-commerce to now supporting mission-critical flows of information for government and business, Mr. Bartkiewicz predicts that the role of today's CIO has never been greater and the business risks of technology failure never more catastrophic. By introducing new ways to think about information economics and information malpractice, *Unseen Liability* offers an extremely valuable perspective to any business or public leader who relies upon, manages, or invests in information technology. This book intrigued me and motivated me as much as it set off alarm bells in my head. Economists, risk managers, CIO's and CEO's would benefit not just by reading this book, but also by striving to balance the emerging information assets and information liabilities within their own organizations.

Recent events such as cyber attacks on Google, lawsuits against Facebook, or breached data in virtually every industry illustrate the trend that we are in new times: exciting times, yet uncertain times. In the worlds of both business and civil society, we are collectively entering the information age with few universal standards of care to guide our technology-born errors, judgments, and liabilities. This emerging reality of ungoverned technology dependence clearly means unseen risks for business and unintended consequences for society.

If the last fifteen years of Internet disruption were any indication, then *Unseen Liability* offers a refreshing and needed reminder that for every positive action, there is an equal and opposite counteraction.

Unseen Liability

Whether we run a business or simply surf the Web, we should all respect not just how quickly technology is changing our world, but continually ask how quickly business can adapt to using this technology wisely and sustainably. Mr. Bartkiewicz's practical and convincing perspective will resonate with any private or public figure who wishes to understand where we have collectively taken technology - and where technology may take us in the future. I believe that *Unseen Liability* will be a book of unusual longevity as its long-term implications are eventually understood and appreciated by technology, business, and civic leaders.

    Dr. Harvey Schiller, Brigadier General Air Force, Retired

Technology makes it possible for people to gain control over everything, except over technology.

— John Tudor

Unseen Liability

Introduction

All of the previous, most pressing matters of the world were simply information problems, and all future problems of the world will be created by information. After more than fifteen years of grappling with the global impact of technology's advance, this belief became both my hopeful conclusion and my cautious warning to others.

For many first-time authors, the writing of a book begins with a sharpening moment, a moment of clarity when years of disconnected events and pervasive thoughts come together for the vision of a book to take shape. It's the moment of realization that the picture drawn by connecting the dots in your mind should be a book and shared with others. Since 1995, the Internet has been both the cause and *accelerant* of making these connections.

In my case, the moment of clarity occurred at a conference I attended in Chicago in 2006. I was the third panelist in a session titled "The Future of Medical Malpractice." In fact, it was the first insurance conference I had attended after spending a decade in the high-tech industry. We three panelists were seated on a stage in a hotel ballroom. Before us sat seven hundred or so business insurance brokers, alternately listening to us and checking email on their Blackberry's. I had participated in technology industry panels over the previous decade, so nothing seemed special about this one.

The first panelist was a medical legal expert. He spoke about the future of hospital general counsels and their role in medical decision-making.

Panelist two was a medical insurance underwriter. Her points revolved around alternative diagnosis sources for doctors and the role that ongoing training would play in treatment alternatives. Suffice it to say, both panelists were discussing improvements in the traditional medical profession as opposed to a fundamental shift in how dependent professionals were on information technology.

Then it was my turn. I was uncertain if the attendees of insurance conferences were similar to those of the technology sector. Briefly and with precision, I described what I saw as a growing threat and liability, not just to the medical industry but to all industries.

"I call it 'information malpractice,'" I began.

Quite noticeably, attendees popped their heads up from their BlackBerry screens as I mashed two words—and two worlds—together. Ironically, even the other two panelists swiveled their heads to look at me. That's when I knew I had touched a nerve: suggested a simple yet

Unseen Liability

provocative premise and merged two previously disparate words that will forever be the property of the information age. It's when I was able to articulate the problem I'd seen brewing for years, the potential downside of the technology revolution—unintended consequences in the wake of rapid innovation, the yet-unseen liabilities of our collective and growing technology dependence.

I am not a Luddite; far from it. I'm a technologist by training and profession, having worked in the technology and software industries since leaving graduate school in 1994. I am a believer that innovative technology generally enhances the world around it, makes things easier, quicker, and simpler. However, it is because I come out of the technology industry that I'm also able to observe the growing problems business has created for itself.

Since my start in the tech sector in the mid-1990s, I saw technology as an industry composed of optimists, pioneers, and risk takers. It has been, and still is, staffed by individuals with passion, vision, and steadfast dedication to the next big thing. What business CIO (chief information officer) or start-up CEO (chief executive officer) could resist the creative products, culture, and ads of our technology industry over the last decade? I was part of that industry both in the US and in Europe, and I relished the experience. This is not a group that allows the potential downside to dampen forward progress (fortunately). Murphy's Law is rarely applied or even considered valid. It is a powerful, marvelous, forward-thinking industry. And it makes little room for what might go wrong.

At least, that's mostly true. I was a technologist working within the innovation vortex at the height of the boom. I spent the late 1990s at BroadVision running a business to implement one-to-one e-businesses in Fortune 500 companies. For a most enjoyable period of time, BroadVision was a darling of Wall Street and industry conferences. The dot-com boom made us believe technology was changing everyone and everything for the better. Enthusiasm for technology enablement and Internet openness was contagious and unchallenged, perhaps a little too much so.

Because I'd had the benefit of working with a broad cross-section of industries within such an accelerated time frame, I occasionally allowed myself to consider the potential downside of this new phenomenon of massive data collection and business interconnectivity. Working closely on data collection strategies for large retailers, banks, and health-care companies, I believe I was one of the few software executives who noticed that as we built the first mega databases of customer information, large numbers of employees—strangers—could access information via

Unseen Liability

computers in many different and often unprotected ways. To call the early years of large-scale data collection "unsecured" was an understatement.

After three years of helping architect personalized websites and profile-rich databases, my career progressed to the next-generation software model, salesforce.com, a pioneering archetype of what later became known as a "cloud provider" or software utility. Having moved myself and my young family to Madrid, Spain, I then traveled to sales meetings across Europe and began to hear the first concerns from more traditional companies about increasingly personal (and valuable) information being "exported" from Spain or France to the US. What a concept. Data exports—highly personal information crossing borders through the medium of the Internet, for which data export laws were barely written or understood. Who actually owned the liability of the Internet? Who could pollute this expanding virtual environment with a data spill? And who would a company sue if its reputation were damaged, its data lost, stolen, or destroyed?

Despite being one of the more passionate fans of the salesforce.com model, I found myself increasingly considering catastrophic scenarios; for instance, Cisco's preferred client list getting loose from the server on which it was stored and emailed all over the eastern seaboard. What laws would be broken, what liabilities created, what impact would be dealt to our collective *trust* in technology's perfection? But within a technology firm, these thoughts were a kind of cultural sacrilege, a betrayal to the spirit of technology innovation; considerations not worthy of deeper evaluation. No, the business was too new and the growth too steep to consider the larger implications of such data transfer governance and what they meant for business risk. Everyone around me, partners and colleagues included, wanted to hear about what was new and great and possible. No one wanted to talk about what could possibly go very, very wrong. I realized the technology industry might not be the right place to make this case.

Insurance, on the other hand, was a sleeper industry, a traditional one, but one with the benefit of a historical perspective deeply rooted in its culture and actuarial tables. With time, this could be an industry that would better consider my growing belief that traditional laws, governance, and insurance were written for a business and social world that would soon no longer exist. Technology was rapidly changing everything, for better or worse, and it was the worst that few business leaders seemed to consider.

Insurance is about thoughtful risk transfer; about being prepared for the worst-case scenario. It's about *hedging* for uncertainty of outcomes. Still, I discovered that even the insurance industry was largely unprepared

Unseen Liability

for what was happening. It was ill informed about the upcoming slips and falls of the information age. Two years ago, I founded (and continue to run) a new business in one of the oldest American insurance companies, The Hartford. I continually analyze and underwrite the downside of websites, databases, software, networks, technology dependency, user behaviors on the Web, and even the state of the Internet environment itself. It is through this prism that I have been able to frame what I see as the biggest challenges facing any business using technology—and, frankly, isn't that almost every business? Is there a business or professional services firm today *not* using technology or *not* present on the Internet in some way, shape, or form? Technology mastery has become an information-age core competency that, when practiced skillfully, has unleashed wealth for many traditional and "new model" companies. Amazon, eBay, Google, Yahoo, and Facebook are examples of companies rich in newly acquired and exponentially growing information assets.

But for every action there is an equal and opposite reaction, and with this new power of technology and information comes great responsibility. Amassing the new commercial wealth of information assets is invariably accompanied by new risks and liabilities. The IT department and its growing IT infrastructure have evolved from support "functions" to a combined central nervous system—*the* concentration of risk for the twenty-first century business; the center of the universe—yet few traditional companies recognize this transformation of liabilities and assets. This is why I call it "unseen liability." It's there, it's growing, and it's just not something most companies have been prepared to identify—yet.

In this book, I will lay out where the unseen liability of information and communication technology is lurking in many business models, processes, and strategies. I'll explore the roots of the problem, the trajectory of its impact, and the nature of the uncertainties for these uniquely twenty-first-century risks. I will suggest that the problem is getting worse by significant leaps as technology's impact continues to accelerate, trampling traditional laws and business norms, and catapulting unspoken volumes of personal data into the industry's next major shift: cloud computing. As every new communication tool emerges, as every personal data event is captured right down to a user's behavior, the magnitude of unseen liabilities grows. This is not a static problem waiting for risk managers, lawyers, economists, and lawmakers to catch up. Technology slips and falls, acts of negligence, and potential abuses are growing every day. In fact, the gap between what a business *can* do with information technology and what society thinks they *should* do grows wider every day. Welcome to the world of information malpractice.

Unseen Liability

I do not advocate going back in technological time. It is my hope that business opts to move forward in a smart fashion, eyes wide open, recognizing the genie that has been unleashed and that there is a potential societal price attached to the future progress all may enjoy. The environment of the Internet and its oxygen of data privacy is our collective environment to protect, monitor, and insure. It is in fact a *public good*, a medium, and an ecosystem through which we can accelerate the advancement of our lives. What I want most is to have readers come to the end of this text with the ability to shrug off the title—that the liability will no longer be unseen, but visible and in the crosshairs of business at it moves forward in the information age. As citizens of the Internet and consumers of technology products and services, we all have something to gain—or lose.

Before we can get there, we have to acknowledge the problem created by our success in the technological field. With emerging trends like Web 2.0, cloud computing, and social media, we have crafted a landscape of new possibilities and unprecedented openness. But these business benefits will not come for free, no matter how inexpensive the technology becomes. Information malpractice is not just a term I dreamt up to get my audience's attention at an industry panel. It is the future of business risk in the age of information. Achieving professional, personal, and commercial success will require a new mind-set, a refreshed paradigm, and recognition that technology has created both unprecedented possibilities and unseen liabilities for all of us.

Chapter 1: A Data Explosion

Computers are useless. They can only give you answers.

— Pablo Picasso

Since the very beginnings of trade and commerce, it has been a commonality that most information exchange between buyer and seller, customer and business, was treated as a discrete, confidential, and almost intimate affair. Trust was earned, not given.

Consider the not so distant history of the local American bank. Banks have been collecting personal information about their customers for decades, harkening back to consultations over a notepad, paper deposit slips, and hand-written applications. The reputations of applicant and banker, buyer and seller, were local reputations, with personal and professional references limited to the confines of the community and the reality of proximity.

Banks large and small managed piecemeal, disconnected snapshots of personal information in random, unstructured, and ultimately inefficient processes that took place without fanfare over the lifetime relationship between client and local banker. "Data collection" was nowhere to be found in the strategic plan, yet banks were the recipients of valuable information regarding their clients: income, investments, payment history, business and family relationships that involved money. Most customers relied only on their local bankers to know them personally and therefore to be capable of making recommendations and offering personalized financial advice. Customer-to-computer interactions, later known as "self-service," were still a fantasy in the minds of fiction writers like George Orwell.

For over a hundred years banks stored their data locally, first in secured filing cabinets, then safes, and as time progressed, on local computers backed up centrally, just as a precaution. By and large the customer relationship and treatment of privacy was based on *local* proximity and *personal* discretion. If a breach of confidentiality occurred, it was entirely local in nature, usually involving only a handful of individuals, with minimal impact to the wider community and certainly little impact on the overall banking institution. The relationship was personal, much like the one embodied by George Bailey, the beleaguered banker in the Christmas classic film *It's a Wonderful Life*. But the landscape of customer

Unseen Liability

information was unique also for cultural reasons and societal norms. *Individuals owned their personal information, not banks.* This distinction is significant given the incredibly electronic world that now surrounds us.

Today, this data scenario and concept of "confidentiality" is as outdated as the black-and-white movie. Client confidentiality is no longer parsed out in handfuls among consenting and trusting individuals with personal and community ties. Few bank customers today live in the world of George Bailey and his town full of customers he knew by their first names. In fact, it is just the opposite. This is not merely the emerging era of data exchange; it is the beginning of the largest personal data explosion the world has ever seen.

What explosion? Consider this handful of statistics, courtesy of data compiled by Forrester Research in 2008:>>

* Internet users share 250 percent more personal data online than they did in 1999.

* 27 percent of enterprises surveyed have fifty or more terabyte production databases.

*50 percent annual growth is reported in online transactional data and repositories.

*The average American company is doubling its volume of customer information every year. This statistic in itself is startling.

The explosion of data is also going international and isn't anywhere near over. Personal data aggregation is only expanding as more health, financial, and social information elements find their way from individuals and businesses into the "clouds" of networked computers, handheld devices, and massive data warehouses. Not only does the business and professional world know how to collect more data, it is also capable of storing it at lower and lower costs. The old days when confidentiality and personal privacy were held in trusted cocoons of discrete individual relationships are over. Data, the lubricant of automating modern commerce, is essentially loose in the digital ecosystem. It is flowing without interruption across physical and legal borders, feeding the data-hungry environment we have created.

Company reputation, personal privacy, and business risk have new meaning and unprecedented exposures. Knowing how to succeed, or fail, in such a cyber world gives cause for a better understanding of the technology blind spots, for individuals and businesses alike. But how did we get here so quickly, and have we fully evaluated the unintended consequences of our technology addiction and Internet openness?

Given that we now have the benefit of looking backward, we can see a convergence of three key forces that accelerated the data explosion:

Unseen Liability

information economics, information technology, and information culture. All three factors have occurred so quickly and in such a parallel fashion that it is difficult to determine which came first or which caused the other.

Information Economics

Look for the core reason behind any major business trend and chances are the trend exists by helping companies radically save costs, grow revenues, or increase the rate of innovation. The data explosion that rode the wave of the Internet is no exception. Despite the initial hype and temporary bust of Web 1.0 (the first generation of the Internet), this new ecosystem for business created substantially new ways to generate wealth and value.

In 2000, I participated with the Brookings Institution in the researching and writing of a new book, *Unseen Wealth*. It assessed the characteristics of new-model companies like Amazon, Dell, Yahoo, and eBay, all of which achieved stunning market valuations without actually making, or even owning, what financiers had long considered traditional book assets. Indeed, the companies of the late 1990s amassing a new form of wealth were a departure from the long-held beliefs inherent in the definition of the word "asset." In many cases, these information-heavy companies managed insignificant physical assets, apart from their real estate, computers, desks, inventory, and the occasional foosball table.

With the exception on-demand manufacturers like Dell, they didn't make anything tangible. In fact, their balance sheets and "book values" were disproportionately matched with their amazingly high market values. The market was valuing these companies on *new* assets: intangible ones not yet fully defined or understood. The technology-agile companies were the high flyers of Wall Street. They were attracting investors in droves and emerging as a driving force in what appeared to be a new market where information technology itself expanded the marketplace of first-time stock buyers. As we learned later, we were all smarter—and dumber—at once. But we did learn something in the process. At least some of us did.

What these types of companies possessed, Brookings determined, were wealth generating "information assets"—previously scarce, unmeasured, and unaccounted for using traditional accounting metrics. These new-model companies leapfrogged their traditional counterparts in being able to know exactly what their customers wanted, what they were buying, and how they behaved on a "personalized" website designed to increasingly collect even more data. At the turn of this century and as a result of tremendous technological advancement a new currency—data—was being collected, processed, managed, and now *valued*. Unseen wealth was not just how much data a business collected but how well they used that data to increase company revenues, cut costs, or innovate.

Unseen Liability

Information economics was in its infancy, but it was also becoming very real to the capital markets and entrepreneurs that moved them.

Thanks to the economics of cheaper data collection combined with higher-value data currencies, this new breed of companies had invented ways to make the standard practice of getting to know your customer into a revenue stream. The surging volumes of personal data—everything from names and addresses to purchasing habits and credit card numbers—emerged as stored assets and the fuel for deeper business intelligence. The real thrust for one-to-one marketing was not just a customer service nicety. It had much longer-term value. Personal data was becoming a critical element in the way these companies made money—and lots of it.

The gradual recognition of information assets—of unseen wealth—unleashed an economic and data-collection frenzy. The humble database, once a sleepy little back-office component in a company, emerged as a prized and mission-critical piece of a company's asset base. Data became currency. Not only could companies leverage data to their own advantage, they could use it to get things of value from other elements of the business world. They could bargain with this data, negotiate with it, trade and sell it. Data was doing more than making money—it *was* money. It was literally the new gold.

Predictably, as the volume, value, and usability of data grew a gold rush ensued. Accountants and analysts moved clumsily to account for the values and quantify them, forging renewed attention and dedication to the "good will" column of company balance sheets, the only remaining location where traditional auditors could estimate this new class of assets. The impact of information economics was felt not just by the dot-com stars, but by traditional enterprises that discovered new data-driven innovations as a result of the information they could collect from their customers. Apple is a good example of one such beneficiary.

Alongside the legitimate commercial interests of information economics lurked the potential dark side of the phenomenon, the blind spot of technology's progress. If confidential personal and company data was truly becoming a valued currency, it stood to reason someone would want to steal it, take advantage of it, or abuse it. And in just three short years, a black market for stolen data emerged, crime rings developed, and companies found themselves with assets they could value and trade—or get sued over.

Despite the potential risks and liabilities, early data privacy breaches and spills did not dampen the enthusiasm for the new asset class. Once identified as valuable and necessary, customer information would never go back to sleepy back-office status at George Bailey's bank. It had

Unseen Liability

moved from the filing cabinet to the asset column, which would soon grow exponentially in volume and value. There was no going back—information technology itself only accelerated our path toward the business of data.

Information Technology

Even with the financial drivers of emerging information economics, the recent data explosion could not have happened without the tidal wave of technology innovation and the equally dramatic drop in technology costs. Business could do so much more with technology than the previous year, and at an incrementally cheaper cost. Data collection and storage technologies, in particular, became dramatic accelerants of business in the information age. Prior to the mid-1990s, it was a costly and common limitation for most businesses to have an aggregate and accurate view of their customers and competitors. Creating a detailed dossier on anyone or anything required volumes of disparate data stored across the multiple touch points of customer interaction. Few companies could manage this technological challenge and its cost barriers. High technology costs and a lack of data collection capabilities were the principle impediments. So, if personal or business data made its way into the enterprise computer, it was mainly unstructured, ad hoc, and not practicable to systematically aggregate.

As we pushed through 2004, the mastery of information technology, especially in concert and openness with the Internet, was becoming a business mandate for creating new wealth and sustainability in the information age. Propelled by conferences, consultancies, and books, one-to-one marketing was the business mantra that drove data collection into high gear. As a result, the combination of information technology infrastructures and learning cultures became the cornerstone for future company growth. It was, in fact, mission critical to the modern enterprise.

But the innovators of the technology industry were not satisfied with that state of affairs, and they turned their attention to creating better, more Internet-based information solutions. The results reconfigured the data storage industry. In 1990, the average cost of one gigabyte of data storage was around $20,000. Today, it is less than $1. The affordability of data storage was radically altered, unlocking a critical path to the information economy. The combination of Internet connectivity and cheaper data storage was irresistible for business. Data in great quantities was in circulation in a new Internet environment. Increasingly valuable, personal data could now be harvested at a fraction of the previous costs. Systematic, robust data collection was a major business thrust from 1995 to today, but the marketplace lacked any standards of how to professionally and legally acquire it, process it, or secure it. Such a lapse in law, regulation, and professional standards left a willing public and their

Unseen Liability

personal data assets exposed. A lack of public awareness of technology's *real* potential, in fact, fed the equally significant transition and creation of an information culture.

Information Culture

None of the massive data aggregation over the last decade could have been possible without the willing and active participation of the Internet masses. This shift in the psyche of the Internet user toward openness and full data sharing cannot be underestimated. What is perhaps most striking is the speed with which the cultural transition occurred. Think back to the early days of e-commerce (only a decade ago!), when consumers were cautious if not hesitant to type their credit card information into an online form, the gray matter of cyberspace. We worried. What would happen to our data? Was it safe to share it? Was the Internet itself safe? Were we taking an unnecessary risk by sharing online? The caution and trepidation with which consumers approached the sharing of data online seems almost quaint by today's standards. Today it is a data free-for-all with little if any consideration given to the downstream impact on personal reputation, identity, or privacy. Amid exploding e-commerce, social media, blogging, and Web 2.0 innovations, we collectively engage in a data orgy in concert with commercial interests, with little professional standards to guide the industry toward sustainability.

Since the decade it took for e-commerce to take hold, consumers have become willing participants in the cultural data explosion. Far from recoiling from it or fearing it, we Internet citizens of 2010 are fueling data warehouses on a daily basis, making very personal donations of data about us, our friends, and our thoughts. In blogs and websites, we chronicle our business and personal happenings. Via services such as LinkedIn, we offer up our resumes, our business contacts, our customer lists, and our networking connections. Then there's the sharing of our social information, which today borders on extreme for the younger generation of eager Internet participants. Users of Facebook and MySpace take data sharing to new heights with personal narratives, rants, photographs, videos, and commentaries. The speed and reach of this online data sharing is only just emerging, as young job seekers find their Facebook pages accessed by would-be employers and no one takes a business meeting without first googling the participants. The online world is awash with data and technology innovators who are continuing to develop newer, faster ways to get us to share even more. Consider Twitter, which affords users a no-cost opportunity to share, share, and share all day long. It is a constant stream of data, from the individual outward into the global

Unseen Liability

clouds. Yet few precedents, laws, or regulations dictate what can happen to that data once it's in the clouds.

With economic, technological, and cultural forces fueling its flames, the data explosion shows no sign of ebbing soon. The question now is not when or how it will end but, more to the point, what will we do now that it's happened? What are the boundaries for commercial ambitions? Political ones? Like an email sent in anger, there is no putting the genie back in the bottle. The technology explosion has occurred and the information age is upon us. In the absence of universal norms, adaptive laws, or standards of care, business and society must now consider, "What's next?"

Chapter 2: A Communications Revolution

In view of all the deadly computer viruses that have been spreading lately, Weekend Update *would like to remind you: when you link up to another computer, you're linking up to every computer that that computer has ever linked up to.*

— Dennis Miller

Few would argue that we live in the midst of a communications revolution. The speed and scope with which we can connect has evolved with the vigor only a science-fiction author might have imagined a decade ago. Devices allow us to share thoughts, images, opinions, news, and experiences across town and across time zones. Individuals can connect and engage anytime, with anyone, across any length of time or space. We are all just clicks away from conversation with our friends, families, customers, partners—or strangers on the other side of the world. The human conversation, digitally enabled and stored forever, is in a new era. It is probably the most fundamental proof that we are at the dawn of the information age. And companies with the digital smarts and ambition now stand to generate significant profits by enabling, fostering, and *listening* to that conversation. The question is, however, what standards of care exist to prevent or even detect professional or personal abuses of this communications explosion?

The expansive and rapid development of communication technologies has had an enormous business impact for industries from retail to health care to financial services, to name a few. Just as individuals can communicate with one another, businesses can communicate with each other, with their employees, and with their customers with ever-evolving speed and one-to-one detail. This culture of connectivity with customers and partners has engulfed the business world with magnificent capital investments in information infrastructures. Never before has the world spent so much on information technology, nor depended so greatly upon its availability. It is a noteworthy warning, however, that such unprecedented connectivity has also fostered a new level of business interdependency, an unchallenged connectivity that we have yet to fully grasp.

Businesses that once operated as islands now exchange real-time data with vendors and suppliers, to speed service and improve efficiencies. The decades old "just in time" business mandate has reached new levels of meaning and reality, to real-time information

Unseen Liability

interdependence. One company's IT operations can automatically impact another, which impacts another, and another, and so on. The domino effect is alive and well in a world where computers *need* other computers, in other companies, to function without interruption.

I began to appreciate this interdependence while working at salesforce.com, a pioneer of cloud computing technology. One business database responds to the data field of another, triggering a multi-server data event to upload, cache, and initiate a call to another database on another continent—all within milliseconds and without the need for the human eye of judgment or interpretation. Computer hardware designed in the 1990s to automate internal business processes is being overridden with hardware and software to operate *externally* on the grid—the World Wide Web—depending ever more on data access to massive "clouds" of business and consumer data. Ironically, if not frighteningly, the technical means of this data exchange via automated programming interface (API) is often managed by lower-lever software employees who are rarely supervised or trained on mitigating the risks of interdependence and systemic data liabilities.

The continual exchange of consumer data with business functions has also grown exponentially in both the *speed* with which date is passed and the *volume* of personal data being exchanged. Business has

39

made a business out of making it increasingly easier to capture personal data—ranging from a user's stated profile to their online behavioral profile, and now even to their social profile—by tapping into online conversations and communications. In fact, detailed "social graphs" of individuals are possible as computers keep watching us. And as communications devices improve and companies learn more about connected citizens, the nirvana of marketing—one-to-one marketing, the symbiotic exchange of information that turns a transaction into a personalized exchange with a machine—becomes ever more attainable. In most cases, the machine (website, kiosk, and cell phone) knows more about you as a digital person than you might like. This fact alone has created uncertainties for the digital person and unseen liabilities for the digital company.

With the number of data privacy breaches growing over the last few years, it is quite possible that we have been lulled into a false sense of comfort, a suspension of our instincts to question. The communications revolution as the Trojan horse of the information age appears purely positive at first blush. And indeed, it is a positive development for our human potential. Many positives of the communications revolution are true. It is a good thing that individuals can connect and share information across time and space. We can collaborate. It is a good thing that business-to-business data flows and transactions are more efficient, more

Unseen Liability

"real time." We are functional, more efficient. It is a good thing that companies can now make faster and smarter decisions about what their customers want and do a better job serving their needs (even if it's the computer making the judgment of what those needs are). We can learn. In fact, when used wisely, and absent any major failures in the ecosystem, this is a potent – if not revolutionary -combination of communications and information technologies. The problem is that professional wisdom / judgment is not always what happens when human variability, commercial economic interests, and laws intersect with technology advancement. The move to technology dependence is largely a self-governing movement thus far, so companies expose themselves to the potential downside of this racing ecosystem without ever knowing the downside.

As is often the case with accelerated societal or commercial transformations, the early glow of the initial paradigm shift can fade, even if just a bit, under more thoughtful scrutiny and consideration of the potential negative and often unintended consequences. Based on what I have researched and witnessed over the last several years, we are at a point where the potential problems with the communications revolution are manifesting into actual problems. They are no longer unseen liabilities.

Two long-held sayings in our society are in need of repeating, in light of our technology dependence and insatiable thirst for personal data.

First, not all communications have positive outcomes and, second, speed can kill. These simple truths, if I may call them such, are especially relevant for businesses that have become so dependant on technology and the open Internet that they are virtually held hostage to the availability of their IT networks and real-time access to their information assets. Such companies have in many ways become data addicts, in need of ever-greater profile information about what their customers say, buy, think, do, and want.

Based on the exponential growth in online search, online marketing, and business intelligence, the commercial appetite for data assets appears relentless. Such a prolongation of intimate customer involvement, therefore, leads commercial enterprises ever closer to the ideal of "one-to-one marketing"—knowing an individual as a digital person and capitalizing on the efficiency of technology and the electronic ecosystem to serve and anticipate their needs automatically, intelligently, and without interruption. With every click and data event, we as users continue to build our own mousetrap.

Perhaps the greatest threat to business out of the communications revolution evolves out of this notion, this quest, and this increasing valuation of one-to-one marketing. One-to-one is an implied contract between consumers and business, clients and professionals. One-

Unseen Liability

to-one on a mass scale, however, runs through technology, networks, and the Internet. Communication and information technologies have made this pursuit a mass-market possibility for the first time ever. As such, abuses of technology or errors in how it is managed can take us quickly from a protected one-to-one relationship to a one-to-many public disaster. Here is where our trust in technology will be tested, where unseen liabilities exist for business and consumers alike. It is when the *many* get negatively involved in the fallout of technology negligence or impacted by a technology error that our sensitivities go into high gear.

Technology dependence and the communications revolution have already created some recent and unusual events in business risk.

Ask WellPoint.

The well-respected health-care company announced in January of 2009 that a technology glitch resulted in their en masse denial of prescription claims to thousands of Medicaid beneficiaries. Critics (yes, many of them bloggers) tell another story. They suggest the firm was lax in its technology management and oversight, thereby denying the claims of millions who suffer from conditions ranging from diabetes to asthma.

Being "cheap with IT," whether it was real or not, suggests that a widely accepted standard of care for technology governance is still up for debate. Because of the communications revolution, it actually doesn't matter what caused the technology error. Bad news spread fast, far, and wide, like a cascading event that blindsided WellPoint. Within hours, WellPoint's actions—the denial of benefits—were out on that global communications platform of the Internet, ripe for comment, rumor, gossip, and judgment.   Whether or not the outage was a conscious action or an innocent software error is no longer relevant. The information age potentiality is that news of unexpected events and fallout can linger in perpetuity in cyberspace. Consequently, truth knows no resting place, fact knows no home, and rumor lives on.

News having a "tail" on the Internet is yet another reality of the participative Internet. This tail is created, manifested, and propagated by both the power and smallness of "we." Risk managers want the bad news to have a short tail while marketing managers want the good news to have a long one. Often the company is quite powerless with its message and increasingly at the mercy of the Internet environment. Blind spots abound and liabilities lurk.

The negative results for WellPoint came swiftly: the company was penalized by Medicaid and forced to halt its acceptance of new Medicaid customers for one month. Customer complaints spiked and lawsuits took form. The one-month interruption in particular was ill timed for the company, which also saw a negative impact to its stock price. WellPoint

Unseen Liability

also had to deal with the harm to its reputation, both for its own business and any businesses with which it may have partnered. News of the problem traveled far and traveled swiftly. Such is the Internet. It all took only a couple of days to unfold. What is noteworthy is that the incident was not only created *by* technology in the form of a failure, but that communication technology *magnified* the problem to the outside world. This is the double-edged sword of the communications revolution, and most companies are learning it the hard way.

Ask eBay.

The online auction company emerged in the late 1990s as a new-model commerce company, purely online and rich in information assets. Never before have so many small merchants and tag-sale junkies been able to connect with so many customers. Thanks to eBay, the truly global marketplace became a reality for many small merchants and consumers. Time and space no longer hemmed commerce. The computer screen became an access point to a worldwide sales bazaar, and both buyers and sellers rushed to participate. By providing this virtual connection point, eBay revolutionized communication between merchant and customer. Both sides of the transaction seemed to celebrate the intersection of scale, bargaining, and convenience as eBay became one of the largest online commerce sites in the world.

Yet even as eBay has become a household name, unseen liability emerged for it as well. Today, eBay battles a barrage of lawsuits from businesses claiming its virtual marketplace has harmed their trademark or their previous distribution networks. Louis Vuitton asserted that eBay merchants repeatedly sold fakes of its branded products on eBay, illegally cashing in on their prestigious French brands and diluting valuable brand assets. Similarly, prepublication book galleys, complete with their NOT FOR SALE stamp, are frequently on the site, confounding publishers and authors who lose out on royalties.

Hollywood fumes when ungoverned Internet users steal, copy, or skim entertainment assets and auction them to the highest bidder. But who is to blame for these increasingly costly technology abuses? Who owns the liability for the wrongful, if not illegal, acts of Internet users? Who pays the price for one firm's lack of technology mastery or reckless display of technology bravado? Some legal and commerce policy experts suggest the fault lies with eBay, which created and profits from its virtual marketplace. But to what extent should eBay be responsible for the damages of the bad actors who found their way online? Courts in different counties have found various ways to view these cases, some courts backing eBay and others siding with the litigious and concerned brand owners.

Unseen Liability

We do not have the luxury of thirty years' experience to establish a more universal standard of care, a more accepted norm for communications and technology guidelines. The information age is just beginning, but the gap between what one business *can* do with technology and what it *should* do is ever widening. As such, the legal status of business versus consumer liability is in flux given the relative newness of so many technology-enabled business processes and models. Such flux in emerging cyber law or Internet norms creates increasing uncertainty for businesses. The social Web elements of Web 2.0 have just raised the stakes as well. In most of the companies that I underwrite for technology risk, many will encounter technology blind spots for infringing on laws or regulations yet to be written.

Ask MySpace.

Like many new companies of the communications revolution, MySpace and its similar one-thousand-plus social site competitors, add yet another angle to business and consumer complexity. The commerce explosion of the Internet has gone social, and it appears to be MySpace's mission to provide tools and data models for others to mass communicate among themselves. Unlike a traditional media or commerce company, MySpace creates almost no original content; it creates an *environment* for users to display their own content. For this it relies primarily on basic terms of use and good judgment to govern that environment. And herein lays the problem. Self-governance often gives birth to bad actors, excessive concentrations of risk, ill-conceived rules, and unintended outcomes. Admittedly, the majority of the 20-million-plus MySpace users adhere to the rules MySpace establishes, but with a high percentage of users seeking ever-increasing ways to be unique, reckless or malicious, unseen liability has emerged for social media businesses – and traditional companies that partner with those businesses.

When two young girls in suburban St. Louis, Missouri, had a very public, online falling out, the mother of one used the MySpace environment to avenge her daughter's hurt feelings. Contrary to the spirit of the MySpace terms of use, the mother entered MySpace posing as a young man. She then engaged her daughter's ex-friend in a virtual friendship, publicly and online, which as many people are learning are one in the same. After several weeks of fostering trust, friendship, and intimacy, the mother had the virtual young man dump the real-life girl with the posted message "the world would be better off without you." A day later the devastated teenage girl committed suicide. Who is guilty? And of what crime? Who is liable in the technology ecosystem, if anyone? MySpace, as a tool in the communications revolution, is drawn into a human conflict that once upon a time would have only involved a few girls, their parents, and maybe the school where such events occurred.

Unseen Liability

Soon this scenario became just one more test case in establishing the fluid and ill-defined boundaries of Internet liability. With the communications revolution have come consequences, and business is being forced to face them in a very public way. This is an example of testing whether MySpace, or any business on the Internet, is liable for the wrongful acts of its users, especially when a user's violation of the terms of use go undetected.

Now what?

In the face of increasing data privacy incidents and Internet-related lawsuits, one can see that technology advancement has outpaced the ability of business and government to establish reasonable or widely accepted standards of care, norms, and even rules. If the last ten years are any indication, the next decade will see an increasingly fast evolution, with tremendous advantages and daunting challenges. For business, the mandate is clear. Industry can acknowledge the blind spots and uncertainties the communications revolution has produced and consider risk transfer methods to deal with the fallout.

Uncertainties during Technology Self-Governance

> *The Internet is so big, so powerful and pointless that for some people it is a complete substitute for life.*
>
> — Andrew Brown

In the absence of established norms or laws, the first step is to address this question: can businesses, consumers, and professionals self-govern their use of technology at such an early stage of the information age?

The answer is all around us. The use of technology for information and communications is essentially self-governing. How this governance is balanced differs among businesses and individuals. For consumers, online communication is governed largely by social and cultural norms. Heavy users of technology and the Internet accept a set of commonly practiced standards and "social courtesies" as the boundaries of their communications and online interaction. They do not use capital letters UNLESS WE WANT SOMEONE TO THINK WE ARE SHOUTING. They use pen names and cryptic emails when they want anonymity. They believe a positive ranking of another's product or service may encourage a similar nod from the beneficiary, a quid pro quo. "Do unto others as you would have others to do unto you" appears to govern some sense of Internet decorum among most thoughtful online users.

Business in the electronic world, however, has its own set of self-governing standards. Its driving force is not societal norms, but business value. The automated communication among businesses, the interdependency, in fact, is driven by the ability of adjoining parties to make money, either by reducing expenses or expanding revenues. Companies like salesforce.com and Facebook may open up their technological platforms and share their intellectual property assets for the ultimate value they may reap down the line. As evidenced by the ever-growing partnerships in cyberspace, many companies have embraced the concept that economic interests will suffice to keep businesses in line and in harmony with each other.

How well has self-governance worked thus far? Well, if the results include widespread privacy breaches, network interruptions, reputation attacks, IP (Internet protocol) infringements, and tragic suicides, perhaps the self-governing method is not the most sustainable one. Certainly, the business environment is not keeping pace with the bad actors who have found the communications revolution a bonanza for theft, IP piracy, slander, and personal injury. And a bad actor can be anyone from an experienced data thief selling personally identifying information on the black market to an individual who abuses anonymity to slander or steal another persons' (or company's) identity and reputation. It can be a professional criminal or a neighbor with a grudge. It can be a technology oversight or a technology failure. Either way, neither societal norms nor the free market enterprise system is creating a safe and legal framework for predictable business online. We are stumbling our way into the information age without formally acknowledging that we have already arrived.

The early legal arguments around unseen liabilities have already trickled their way into the court system, but few people have connected the dots that these liabilities were created by, related to, or exacerbated by technology. In fact, none of these recent, high profile events would have occurred without technology. Even the resolution of early individual cases does not promise a sustainable framework as the communications revolution continues to expand. New ways to communicate and new ways for bad or unintended communications emerge with every passing business cycle. The growing docket of courtroom filings and sensational headlines clearly indicates that self-governance may not be sufficient to manage the communications revolution in a business-friendly environment.

As much as we may all dislike the concept of new regulations or laws, information age participants, both commercial enterprises and individuals, may benefit from a more thoughtful set of technology standards in order to move forward in a profitable and sustainable way. Settling for a case-by-case standard of rules and regulations is piecemeal, slow, and not even practical given the diversity of technology risks now in play. Businesses and individuals are exposed in ways they may not even realize. Waiting around for each case to be settled is hardly a workable solution, but will likely be the environment for the next several years. And it is for that reason that professionals are exposed to uncertainty.

We are in a cycle of innovation that also breeds a cycle of unintended consequences, of risks and liabilities that indirectly or directly result from that innovation. New liabilities are right around the corner because new technology developments are equally right around the corner. A gap is being created by the fact that the virtual world is continually out of synch or ahead of the physical world. What you *can* do with technology is outpacing the norms, laws, and standards of what you *should* do with technology. If there is one thing we have learned from the last decade it is that. New technologies and new *uses* for technology give birth to new and often unseen business risks and liabilities. Business leaders in this next decade need better awareness, measurements, frameworks, and risk products to navigate the wave of uncertainty and respond by better protecting their businesses.

Certainly, there are those who will fret that any system of regulation or a more universal definition of information malpractice will kill the communications revolution in its tracks. To them I would respond: the communications revolution is still in its infancy and thinking about ways to make it more sustainable benefits business and users alike.

Overindulgence or abuse of the revolution's openness by a small percentage of players can ruin it for the majority of information age participants that see the enormous benefits for innovation and growth, for sharing and collaborating. Analogous to what I mean by this concentration of risk, we learned this lesson the hard way in the 2008 credit crisis and ensuing financial collapse. The irresponsibility of a few fed the overindulgence of a minority, which then brought down the system for the majority.

Is comparing an impending privacy crisis to the credit crisis too big a leap? Consider this. The promise of one-to-one marketing, of the communications revolution itself, is predicated on the consumer's willingness to share personal data, images, opinions, and activities. No consumer relationship management (CRM) or social media application can produce the necessary data to create perfectly designed products, services, and marketing messages unless consumers are willing to contribute their information, their *trust,* to the process. So far, most online users are willing to take this leap with businesses and with each other in an exploding online social environment. But how long will that last if people no longer trust the intentions of those securing the data, those accessing the data, or the security of the Internet environment itself? Without greater awareness of the consequences of data "overshares" or

Unseen Liability

"data spills," we run the risk of an Internet citizenry with massive data and reputational hangovers down the road.

To continue to expect individuals (yes, consumers!) to participate, companies must reinvent the notion of privacy and demonstrate a "good citizen" approach to new professional standards and accountability in the information age. People will only continue to share their opinions, personal attributes, product rankings, and content online as long as they can be assured of a reasonable backdrop of privacy and security, of respect for their reputation and name. *Public trust in the Internet has become the driving force of the communications revolution; business is at risk of squandering this asset by being unaware of its very real technology blind spots.*

Routinely if not daily, news appears in major media highlighting a data leak or privacy breach of some kind. Credit card companies report breaches to their systems. Government institutions report stolen laptops. Private companies discover their customer lists have been hacked. Already, consumers are starting to wonder if all this data sharing is such a good idea. Just as financial services ran into hard times when trust in the credit markets eroded, the same future may be in store for the Internet environment if the public trust is squandered, ignored, or underestimated. If trust in the communications revolution falters, individuals and businesses will back away. The virtual marketplace and social media landscape will shrink. The global human conversation will fade. The many ways in which communication technology has enhanced business and individual expression will diminish.

This radically new social and business environment of the open Internet—Web 2.0—offers us new paths for innovation, collaboration, and a real reason for optimism. We are certainly in a data-driven and network-dependent economy, but we can't rely on a set of emotionally driven systems to guide us forward indefinitely. Nor can companies fly even higher within this environment without considering the risks and the downside. As in all previously significant commercial evolutions, visionaries must eventually identify the practicalities and reach consensus on those elements that can be sustained in a more predictable and legal economic environment.

Unseen liability states firmly that law, technology, and business risk are rapidly converging to establish the longer-term Internet and technology boundaries. In essence, through current mishaps and case law, we are at the dawn of defining a new term: "information malpractice." Without a discussion or understanding of this notion, businesses and users alike may find it's safer to retreat from the information age and leave their economic and reputational destiny in the hands of others.

Chapter 3: The Emergence of Technology Blind Spots

It has become appallingly obvious that our technology has exceeded our humanity.

— Albert Einstein

To understand the nature of the growing risks facing the technology-dependent business world, consider the following stories recently found in business newswires.

On a September morning in 2008, the normally steady shares of United Airlines (UAL) began to free-fall. Within minutes, shares of UAL lost 75 percent of their value as investors and company officials scrambled to figure out what was going on. The source of the drama, it turned out, was a news story reporting UAL had filed for bankruptcy protection. The problem was that story was from 2002. United had successfully emerged from bankruptcy protection in 2006. The *Chicago Tribune*'s 2002 article had been archived and on that morning in 2008, retrieved by a search engine, and treated as fresh news. Although UAL was eventually able to detect the problem and relay the accurate information to the markets, it could not give a good estimate as to how much money was lost in the scuffle.

One of the most popular Internet companies to come down the pike is YouTube, the video-sharing website where users can upload, view, and share video clips. Three former PayPal employees created YouTube in February 2005. The company estimates more than 65,000 new videos are uploaded every day, and that the site logs 100 million video views per day. But YouTube has hit a hurdle in its success story, given the fact that intellectual property laws have not kept pace with online users' ability to stretch them. Although it's hard to say exactly how much, a big part of YouTube's success is derived from the fact that many of the uploaded videos are not entirely original user content. Many users make their own videos, but many more post and therefore distribute videos made by others, violating en masse others' copyrights in the process.

Viacom, an established and powerful media giant, at first spent significant time and effort simply policing and alerting YouTube to the IP violations on their site, requesting the videos be taken down. But the process became so widespread, so viral, that Viacom could not keep up with the monitoring of infringements. As the site grew in popularity, advertisers flocked to YouTube. The benefits of the newer technology model for YouTube were high, but the costs of the IP dilution felt by

Unseen Liability

Viacom were also high. Technology's speed has created an environment of windfall gains and windfall losses. Such shifts in assets, wealth, and control forced Viacom to go court for a $1 billion lawsuit, asserting that it was the responsibility of YouTube to prevent the massive copyright violations.

It has thus far been a scenario of windfall gains for one new business model and windfall losses for an older one, made possible by a time lag between technology advancements and outdated laws, business standards, and societal norms. And herein lays the reason we are in a period of transition, a period of turbulence, and a period of blind spots. What a company *can* do with technology is outrunning the pace of what a company *should* do with technology, thus creating risk profiles for businesses that are much more dynamic than in previous decades.

In both cases cited above, the firms enjoyed the financial benefits of technology enablement, data aggregation, and the communicative Web. But blind spots were in their midst. The *Chicago Tribune* clearly thought that archiving its old stories was a standard practice, until one surfaced in a way that cost another company significant reputation harm and market losses. Blind spots can be sudden. Perhaps YouTube did not foresee the disruption that its very premise—the free and open posting of video content—could create a problem for a media industry giant and drag YouTube into court. Blind spots can be expensive.

The blind spot of technology dependence is not your ordinary business challenge. It can be a monster that grows and seethes for some period of time before leaping onto the scene with a devastating impact. When companies come face to face with their blind spots, they are generally not small events, but full-scale catastrophes that have been brewing for months, even years, before wrecking their havoc. A hallmark of the experience is the moment when the participants turn to one another and say, "How could this have happened?"

blind spot –noun 2. An area or subject about which one is uninformed, prejudiced, or unappreciative.

—Dictionary.com

Business would be wise to reacquaint itself with the term. It is going to come up a lot in this next phase of our global technology expansion, as errors occur with greater speed and broader impact. Blind spots may be the single fastest growing reality of this stage of the Internet, often referred to as Web 2.0. As the Web 2.0 environment becomes less of a platform for company-controlled content and more of an environment for millions of unregulated users, more and more firms will find that their success is tagged with a host of blind spots, poised to emerge and make themselves known. As UAL and YouTube have found, blind spots can be hazardous to a business's financial health, viability, and reputation. The last three years of claim activity indicate record numbers of data privacy breaches, intellectual property disputes, and other Internet-born business disputes. The common thread among the claims is that they have been created by, related to, or exacerbated by the use of technology. They are all the seeds of information malpractice, so businesses need to strategize, organize, and protect themselves from blind spots of the information age. In fact, one could suggest that many organizations for wealth creation need different models, strategies, and management models to adapt to the competitiveness and risks of the information age.

How did these blind spots develop over the last decade, and why have we not seen this connection sooner? A confluence of trends, which we will look at in detail, has occurred over the last several years:

1. Corporate leaders opted to be technology ignorant.
2. Technologists enjoyed working in the dark.
3. Consumers were happy and unaware.

Corporate leaders opted to be technology ignorant.

Men have become the tools of their tools.

— Henry David Thoreau

When a company's technology systems were easy to understand, many corporate executives were reasonably involved, engaged enough to be conversant. But in the last decade, technology boomed in scope and complexity. Many corporate leaders found themselves relying more and more on IT professionals to understand their companies' technology needs and to pursue and implement solutions. The longer this went on, the more divorced the C-suite became from its IT operations. Two languages for two different worlds evolved. At the higher levels of management there is a general reluctance to admit or address what you don't understand, and this makes the technology blind spot even more of a threat. Company executives were making decisions without addressing or even realizing the business risks manifesting within their increasingly critical IT infrastructures. What a CIO saw as "economies of scale" for centralized server stacks, consolidated databases, and co-located IT services, a risk officer would see as an enormous concentration of risk.

This is not to say the C-suite ignored technology. Indeed, during the dot-com bust greater attention was paid by executives to their technology spending, but it all revolved around the concept of return on investment (ROI). The focus was primarily on revenues, innovation, and

Unseen Liability

growth and far less so on potential risks and unintended consequences. If a technology investment or development project could show ROI, executives would often stop asking questions. This ROI-driven business climate left the more significant blind spots free to languish in obscurity—for a while. If corporate executives had a prejudice, it was born from the prevailing mind-set that technology enablement would yield increased revenue and lower costs, without adding to the company's overall risk profile. In most cases, technology enablement and data dependency did not only alter the risk profile for business, it redefined it. Errors of the information age would go from the contained events of one-to-one human error to the viral events of one-to-many technology catastrophes. Few participants and stakeholders in this emerging ecosystem saw this shift coming, especially the technologists who believed technology itself was an undeniable and unchallengeable advancement for commerce.

Technologists enjoyed working in the dark.

> *The goal of computer science is to build something that will last at least until we've finished building it.*
>
> — Anonymous

Truth be told, IT professionals were not all that unhappy with the way senior management divorced themselves from the subject of information technology management. Many IT department managers and even CIO's liked operating with relative autonomy. Who could blame them? As technology became more complex and more vital to business success, the status of IT professionals soared. They became mission-critical players, individuals whose talents were increasingly valued and coveted. The less corporate executives understood about the technology, the more powerful IT leadership became. It was a heady period for the industry of IT professionals; they were the up-and-coming architects of the *business of information* and the world of technology dependence.

What's more, technologists approached their industry's challenges with their own set of prejudices. In this case, I would frame it as an inflated, if not irrational, blind affection for technology. IT professionals, when faced with any problem or business hurdle, were likely to come up with an answer that involved—you guessed it—more technology. There was "nothing technology could not solve," and so the technological Web expanded and became even more complicated, more interconnected, and more exposed to catastrophic errors. When technologists set out to solve a business problem, their biased answer was almost always "more technology." As they operated in their isolation and irrational exuberance, their blind spot for technology risks continued to grow. **Consumers were happy and unaware.**

Unseen Liability

The Internet is the first thing that humanity has built that humanity doesn't understand, the largest experiment in anarchy that we have ever had.

— Eric Schmidt

Finally, a key component in the evolution of technology blind spots has to be consumers and Internet users. Today, most people who understand the growing privacy and reputation concerns would acknowledge that we, as an Internet society, lagged in our awareness of how vulnerable we were becoming. Think back to the early years of the Internet when individuals worried about the "safety" of typing a credit card number into an e-commerce site. Now it's so common that we are annoyed if the sites we frequent do not have the number stored for us. If we have to go through the motions of actually opening our wallets, we are put out. In addition to accelerating the spread of our credit card data, a far more significant threshold has been passed. We eagerly share personal data for something in return. We willingly trade attributes, interests, and details about ourselves with the expectation of better deals, more convenience, and more intimacy. We are active traders in the marketplace of personal data. We intuitively know that our data has value, yet we are ignorant about the rules of the marketplace and the length of the commitment we are making to cyberspace. The sea change in how we are willing to share our most personal data is enormous. And as long as we are content with this new notion of greater data convenience and the potential for "better deals" and "more temptations," the companies who sell us goods and services are happy too.

In retrospect, we as consumers may have inadvertently numbed ourselves to a massive blind spot for technology. We have fallen in love with it. We have adopted it in all aspects of our lives, business and personal, often mixing the two uses without a second thought. Today, we can't imagine our existence without multiple email addresses, personalized search engines, and intimate e-commerce sites. We do not care to revisit our old fears about online privacy or reputation risk because our level of trust is so high in the companies, the medium, and the environment. We are at a stage where our ability to simply opt out of the information age is virtually impossible. We are addicted to the system and the system knows it.

Even when faced with a direct question about online privacy, there was a period during which most consumers said they were comfortable with their level of exposure. A study conducted in 2006 by the Pew Internet Life Project called Digital Footprints found 60 percent of Internet users were "not worried" about how much information was available about them online. Similarly, the majority of online adults (61 percent) did not feel compelled to limit the amount of information that could be found about them online. Just 38 percent said they had taken steps to limit the amount of online information available about them. Forty-three percent of online adults said they neither worried about their personal information nor took steps to limit the amount of information that could be found out about them online. Just as recently as 2006, the Internet seemed like a friendly environment to us, like a cocktail party where we were among friends. The notion that we might be exposing ourselves to risk was only a minor concern. We didn't put much thought into it and we didn't demand the companies that serve us do either.

But all that has begun to change. Businesses are in the crosshairs of technology risk because their customers are equally in the crosshairs. Technology arrogance and technology ignorance are on a collision course for stirring a deluge of legal arguments the world has yet to ponder.

Companies old and new (like United Airlines and YouTube), startled by experiences of massive data losses, IP infringements, and Internet brand disasters, are starting to reexamine their technology uncertainties, not just from a revenue perspective but from a risk perspective. What was once a sidebar issue in the business world is quickly moving front and center to boardroom-level consideration. Data leaks that were once a page 7 article are now blasted across the headlines, from the Web to television.

The Internet "tail" for technology incompetence is getting longer by the day. Companies are starting to lose real money and lawsuits are coming fast. In today's world, the concept of technology risk is not just an IT concern but a shareholder one. Corporate executives are realizing that their organizations' technology blind spots cannot be ignored or discounted. The economics of technology failure, negligence, or abuse are too great.   We operate in a business environment where technology interdependency is entrenched and blind spots can impact stock prices. Marketing needs to understand if its technology-driven email program violates spam regulations and if it is legally collecting data in accordance with international laws, user understanding, and new regulations. Brand managers need to understand and address how their brands—no, *reputations!* - are exposed by massive online opinion. Public relations need to be in the loop so that when technology-related issues emerge, they are prepared to respond in a way the information age demands. CFOs need to budget or insure for a major data privacy breach, network outage, or business interruption. General counsels need to consider IP exposures of their employees now "publishing" on internal company intranets and external Web 2.0 sites. And the list goes on. Departmental silos are no longer sustainable when it comes to technology blind spots. Because

Unseen Liability

technology is so interwoven into every facet of business behavior, there is no place for a business leader to hide.

Consumers too are recognizing that they can no longer afford to give the technology in their lives a free pass. Consumers may be willing to fall in love with an innovation, but they'll turn on it quickly if the process fails to please or *fails to protect*. As more data breaches continue to make the news, consumers are waking up from their data slumber. Just as Viacom grew tired of policing YouTube's enabling of alleged copyright violations, consumers are increasingly unwilling to bear the brunt of data leaks by the business community. When a company leaks consumer data, consumers want more than a letter of acknowledgment and an apology. They want that company to step up and make them "whole," whatever that means depending on the type of data compromised. Consumers want their data hosts, which today is almost every business, to pay for credit monitoring. They want them to invest in better data security. In some cases, they want them to *pay* for their lack of concern, oversight, or care for their most trusted possessions: their reputation and identity.

Recent consumer awakening, and in some cases ire, have given birth to new privacy regulations. Now forty-four states have instituted data privacy laws, a sure sign that voters are calling their representatives and demanding action. As consumers, we are increasingly unwilling to tolerate the blind spots. We want them fixed because we are the ones who pay the price and bear the burden of data uncertainty.

This confluence of business risk and growing consumer demands has led to a novel concept for the practice of information technology: standards of care. Stakes are being placed in the ground to determine reasonable guidelines for operating a business online, for collecting personal data, for protecting the IP's of others, and for protecting the long-term health of the Internet environment. This means that organizations can no longer be willfully ignorant of their technology risks, nor can they operate their businesses without understanding new laws that relate to technology governance. Such standards of care are important to provide the goalposts for technology success and the penalties for information and technology malpractice. The subject of information malpractice will be addressed fully in the next chapter.

As a society, we have cultural agreements around standards of care that allow us to conduct predictable professional services and deliver reliable business processes. If an individual walks into a hospital or sits down in a classroom or steps onto a public transportation vehicle, that person has an expectation of the standard of care for the provision of that service. This standard is based upon years of previous professional experiences and business best practices because industries like health care,

Unseen Liability

education, manufacturing, banking, accounting, and transportation have been around for decades. These industries have the benefit of time to govern their business practices.

Long-term experience is not the case with information technology, which is a relatively young industry and ripe for catastrophic errors, omissions, and unintended consequences. As a function of the relative newness of technology enablement, blind spots emerge because in most cases the business or professional error that occurred lacks a similar precedent. This is one reason why blind spots can be expensive for a company to defend. The standard of care for such a unique scenario may have yet to be written.

What can a consumer expect from a company with access to his or her credit card? What can a company demand from a vendor of a technology product or service that interrupts not only their business but also the business of their networked partners? What is the responsibility of a new-model Internet company to the previous generations in its industry? What is the liability of a company that improperly sells personal data? What is the liability of a company that inadvertently loses personal data? What laws, and of what country, would even apply? These are the new blind spots that will eventually lead to more universal and well-understood standards of care. But for now, the gap of technology enablement (what can be done) and technology governance (what should be done) is broad. The risk for businesses in the short term is to not be in the crosshairs of a legal argument that tries to establish the standards of care based on technology error or ignorance.

Men obey laws such that they may be free.

— Cicero

Thus far, however, at least some of the debate around the standards has centered more on access and cost of Internet technologies than around risk. In a 2008 article by officials at the Pew center, "Whither the Internet?" the authors reported on a survey of attendees at the Internet Governance Forum.

Here are some of the results:

- Respondents indicated strong support for the establishment of a global Internet users' bill of rights. Some 66 percent agreed with the statement "a global internet users' bill of rights should be adopted." Only 6 percent disagreed.

- Key planks of the bill of rights would be freedom of information, freedom of expression, and the right of people to have affordable access.

- A plurality of participants declared that access to the Internet is the top issue facing global policy makers.

Unseen Liability

- Access was named the top issue in Internet governance today; Internet security came in fourth.

Personal and business risk, it seems, is not yet the dominant issue surrounding the global discussion regarding the Internet. Access remains top of mind. That suggests many businesses are still operating with technology blind spots. It will take more action, more headlines, and more technology-born mishaps before light shines for those users.

If the business world has managed through many decades to maintain its separate organizational and physical silos, that era is ending. Technology has worked its way into every aspect of business and so the era of interdependence is at hand; the concept of unseen liabilities is now real. The business world cannot turn back, nor can it unravel itself from its current trajectory of technology dependence and broad participation on the Internet. We are collectively too far along. The risk, and ensuing liabilities, have already been created. It is simply a matter of time before businesses are forced to identify and quantify their technology-related risks and unintended consequences—and deal with the impact.

Chapter 4: The Birth of Information Malpractice

The danger from computers is not that they will eventually get as smart as men, but that we will meanwhile agree to meet them halfway.

— Bernard Avishai

At the start of this book, I related a story about my first public use of the phrase "information malpractice" at a forum for insurance professionals. The term got an immediate reaction. In this chapter, I'll dive more deeply into the concept of information malpractice to reveal how it can come about for any modern business, large or small. I'll also explain why many companies are much closer to committing information malpractice than they realize and what some of the consequences may be. Like an object in a car's side mirror, information malpractice may be closer than it appears.

mal·prac·tice [mal-prak-tis] –noun

1. Law. Failure of a professional person, as a physician or lawyer, to render proper services through reprehensible ignorance or negligence or through criminal intent, esp. when injury or loss follows.

2. any improper, negligent practice; misconduct or misuse.

—Dictionary.com

In the medical world, malpractice focuses fault on the medical professional (doctor, nurse, administrator) for a "less than standard" treatment of a patient for an illness or injury. There are a few more negative terms one could use for medical professional failures or oversights but this is the most direct and simple explanation. Given the often high stakes of medical treatment missteps, professionals in this industry cannot "practice" health care without widely accepted standards, rigorous guidelines, professional certifications, quality controls, and, yes, insurance. Medical mistakes, omissions, or even intentional acts can cost lives, reputations, careers, and of course money. Annual figures from multiple sources, both private and public, regularly estimate the medical malpractice industry as a multibillion-dollar marketplace. Clearly, this is one industry where insuring for mistakes makes financial sense.

In the business world, "information" and "technology" are almost always words associated with positive, if not neutral, connotations. As a combined term, "information technology" is often associated with efficiency, knowledge, scale, access, and growth. To date, there are few negative associations for the term, yet information is the lifeblood of the

Unseen Liability

modern business or professional organization. Information technology is the central system that pumps this blood.

I brought the two words together to make a point. On one hand, information is the new oil, a lubricant for efficiency, collaboration, and commerce. On the other hand, information is the new *oil*, a business liability if one pollutes the digital environment with information irresponsibly. Business and professional organizations alike need to understand that the *practice of* and *reliance upon* information technology have very real downsides, an unmistakable and unique set of vulnerabilities. Businesses that *need* information and businesses that *broker* information have a whole host of possible negative outcomes, most of which become downstream liabilities to unsuspecting third parties (customers, partners, employees). So, can information malpractice lead to professional liabilities such as a bodily injury? It already has. Can information malpractice lead to another's reputational harm or advertising injury? It occurs almost every day. Can information malpractice cause a third-party economic loss or liability? Yes, without a doubt.

A significant line in business has been crossed, in fact. As a society, we are increasingly unable to really tell where human error ends and technology error begins. We are moving from professional judgments to technology algorithms, from a person-to-person world to a person-to-machine environment. The result is leading to a growth in information malpractice cases (yet to be collectively defined that way) that are already more complex and expensive than their more traditional medical malpractice counterparts. Yet how many businesses or professionals are actually insured for information malpractice and technology mishaps? My estimate is less than 10 percent. Ignorance of the exposure prevails, but this perception is changing rapidly with every headline that relates to yet another technology-created failure, abuse, or incident.

A New Kind of Professional Standard

Doctors clearly don't enter the medical profession to engage in medical malpractice. Still, they insure themselves for significant amounts of money against the possibility. In fact, the average hospital is insured annually for several millions of dollars in medical malpractice insurance. Risk managers, however, are out of step with their CIOs. When was the last time you met a CIO who said they and their business were insured for information malpractice, technology liability, and Internet risk? From the perspective of an underwriter, these risks are not only becoming more common but each exposure is building upon the previous one. The result for most businesses is a risk profile that has grown in both frequency and severity.

Unseen Liability

Leaders of businesses and public and nonprofit organizations increasingly operate in the information economy with speed, investment, agility, and confidence. The modern business depends on data, networks, software, computers, the Internet, and an ever-expanding number of handheld communication devices. In most cases, business does not insure itself against this increased technology dependency and unprecedented concentration of data risk. Even the best doctors can envision an instance in which malpractice may occur, but this is not so in most businesses and professional industries. From my experience in both the technology and insurance industries, business is in denial or ignorant of these unseen liabilities, operating with irrational confidence in technology and little awareness that technology risk transfer is a possibility.

When one makes the connections to what causes information malpractice, one has the benefit of realizing that it can gradually sneak up on a company. It's a state that can arise out of what was originally a positive development, such as a new technology or a new business model enabled by technology. The threat of information malpractice is especially great in these situations because most of the players involved are blinded by their celebration of the new technology or new revenue model; they are largely unaware of what privacy, advertising, and IP laws they may be trampling. They have negligence exposures not only for errors in technology performance but also error in professional judgment in *applying* that technology. This is the most fertile ground for information malpractice to take seed.

The positive assertion to this trend is that like most other business risks, the exposures of information malpractice can be mitigated and when needed, transferred against a financial / insurance backstop to avoid catastrophic liabilities. But that can only happen if companies are willing to acknowledge the possibility and heed the warning signs.

Different Forms of Information Malpractice

Because technology has become so pervasive in commerce, culture, and the delivery of professional services, there are identifiable and subtly different forms of information malpractice. I have categorized these nuances into four categories:

1. Information crimes
2. Information accidents
3. Information ignorance
4. Information arrogance

See if you recognize your company in any of the following scenarios. Some are more obvious than others.

You may be headed for information malpractice if:

You or an employee of your company has committed an **information crime**; that is, the intentional and malicious abuse of

Unseen Liability

information technology to violate an existing law, statute, or professional ethic. Here are some examples:

- Theft of personally identifying information (PII)
- Theft of company confidential information (CCI)
- Extortion for PII
- Extortion for CCI
- Illegal sale of PII
- Theft of intellectual property (IP)
- Insertion of malicious codes or viruses to harm others
- Knowingly creating or propagating false or harmful information online
- Destroying data needed for a regulatory or litigation event
- Knowingly violating any law with information technology as an enabler or accelerator.

That one appears easy, though it is always a fine line as to whether the business knew of an information crime or *should have known* that an information crime was taking place with their employees, on company computers, or via company provided Internet access. Even business owners enamored with technology know that if they commit a crime through the medium of technology or allow that crime to be committed through their neglect of technology, they have put their company into a position where it would likely be liable for damages. No argument there.

However, many business leaders figure that if they or their employees haven't done anything on the above list—that is, committed an information crime—they are clear of any potential liability like information malpractice. But I'll argue that's a blind spot: a false sense of security. Just because you or your employees haven't committed an established crime does not mean your company has not committed information malpractice. Cyber crime is only one possible trigger of information malpractice; there are others.

Often, information malpractice is the culmination of a series of technology-related events. Companies wander into this bog by engaging in technology missteps that may seem harmless at first but can snowball into a malpractice situation. If you didn't identify any exposures for your business on the cyber crime list, congratulations. But you're not out of the woods yet. Consider that your information malpractice event may be

Unseen Liability

brewing deep inside other events in the company—events that don't seem so worrisome at first.

You may be headed for information malpractice if . . .

You have suffered an **information accident**. What's that? Here are a few examples:

- A hardware failure that led to data loss for a third party
- A software glitch that led to the improper distribution of personally identifying information (PII)
- A programmer omission that resulted in a failure in IT security, exposing the networks and valuable information of third parties
- The unintentional transmission of a virus via an email or website link that led to significant data corruption, negatively impacting companies you do business with
- A network outage and ensuing server interruption that caused a business interruption for a partner or client, resulting in lost commerce and profits
- The loss of a backup tape that triggered a data privacy spill and ensuing investigation

The above list, perhaps, is looking more familiar to most businesses. It's a list of increasingly common IT incidents over the last few years. In other words, these are information *errors* and *omissions* whose consequences are increasingly broad and likely to impact one to many businesses at once. The news is that the seeds for information malpractice are being planted every day, with every error and technological misstep, from one industry to another. Most business and consumer relationships have moved to a "self-service" economy where customers use we sites, kiosks, and handheld devices to conduct their interactions. Any one of these information accidents can result in downstream harm to a large number of individuals or damage or loss to another business. This high-volume, catastrophic event is the new liability of the information age, and it is not going away any time soon. Information malpractice has been born and its ability to have broad implications is significant, given the speed and "irreversibility" of most events.

Unlike the Internet of 2000, today's Web 2.0 Internet has created an irreversible web of technology openness, interconnectivity, and interdependence. As the state of technology interdependence expands and weaves businesses together in a tight web of connectivity, these "accidents" can quickly become disasters—viral—in all the wrong ways. During the 1990s, when businesses were still their own islands of IT operation, a power failure or software glitch could do little more than harm the one company. Today, that harm has the potential to multiply exponentially. Yesterday's information accident can be tomorrow's claim for information malpractice. Because we are all connected, business and individuals alike, our responsibility to one another is greater and our errors and accidents are no longer our own.

If you are careful about avoiding information accidents and you hire the right people to minimize committing an information crime, are you and your business safe from information malpractice? I'll argue, no. There are still many ways to be exposed. And the fact that a company considers itself above or somehow uniquely isolated from the threat is one of them. These are what I call the judgment errors—ignorance and arrogance—that lead to information malpractice:

You may be headed for information malpractice if . . .

You have engaged in **information ignorance**. The more technology is embedded in day-to-day business, the less senior executives may know about the IT system and resulting exposures. Senior executives have been very willing to challenge and evaluate IT based on its cost and ROI, but so far less willing to challenge IT investment on the liability and business risk it may be creating. Corporate leaders rely on their IT departments to understand and manage the technology. And since, as we've discussed, the technologists are often decidedly pro-technology in their outlook, the concept of liability is rarely raised. At most it is an afterthought. Technology to the pure technologist is a faith, an unwavering confidence to solve technology problems with more technology.

With this dynamic present in many companies, the topic of IT risk is left in dangerous isolation, almost as a separate discussion that often never occurs within an enterprise. Company management may have an information malpractice blind spot due to a lack of understanding of its company's current technology relationship and be completely unaware of the implications of risk, abuse, neglect, or failure. The more that technology is embedded throughout the company, the more likely technology becomes the critical path to marketing, public relations, sales, support, and operations. This lack of understanding means that information ignorance poses a real danger.

What does information ignorance look like? Some examples:

- A company is unaware that irresponsible employee behaviors on company computer systems or the Internet may create a liability for the company.

- A company is unaware of US and international data collection and protection laws.

Unseen Liability

- A company is unaware of notification laws for a data privacy incident.

- A company is unaware of the libelous or harmful content by users, members, or subscribers of the company website.

- A company is unaware of Internet IP regulations such as DMCA (Digital Millennium Copyright Act) or child protections laws such as COPPA (Children's Online Privacy Protection Act).

- A company is unaware of the amount of PII it has and who has access to it.

- A company is unaware of the latest threats to servers, databases, and IT infrastructures.

- A company does not heed warnings of software and hardware vendors for regular patch management.

- A company is unaware of the latest anti-spam and email laws.

- A company is unaware of the amount of CCI it has aggregated and who has access to it.

- A company is unaware of the extended liabilities of employees online, on social media, blogs, personal emails, etc.

- A company is unaware if is liable for its selection of IT providers and vendors that do not comply with industry guidelines for data privacy and security.

Then there is a final precursor to information malpractice. It is the kind that can likely cause the most trouble for a company. This is **information arrogance**. This kind of technology bravado is what allows otherwise intelligent executives to lead their employees and shareholders into a potential debacle of professional risk and business liability. Information arrogance is what happens when management and IT leaders do not challenge the *implications* of technology and instead simply jump on the bandwagon. Without the checks and balances of an external legal or moral viewpoint, technologists alone are not likely to engage in the exercise of predicting potential liabilities. Businesses or individuals so enamored with cutting-edge technological advancement may not be willing to even imagine the possible downsides of misuse or errors, of pollutions of the Internet, of pushing legal boundaries, of unintended consequences, and dilution of public trust in technology itself.

What does information arrogance look like? It's not hard to spot.

- The company collects data in hidden, unstated, nebulous ways, pushing the envelope of what is acceptable.

- The company has no CPO, CSO, or owner of privacy and security matters, not wanting to assume the cost of better technology governance.

- The company has not established a process to respect user preferences for privacy, underestimating the sensitivity for privacy in different segments, communities, states, or even countries.

- The company lacks a way to continually monitor site content for potential intellectual property infringement, selectively enforcing its terms of use, or understaffing for protections of IP.

- The company is not monitoring its site for potential fraudsters or bad actors, choosing to stand behind their website's terms of use agreement that is untested in courts of law.

- The company lacks a contingency plan to manage a data privacy incident, unwilling to create a record of acknowledgment of any shortcomings.

- The company has no board-level understanding and oversight of technology risks, choosing to minimize the risks of technology on the bottom line.

- The company does not purchase business insurance to cover technology liabilities and unbudgeted technology failures, opting to spend more on technology to benefit revenues, but putting customers, suppliers, and employees at risk for potential abuses, failures, and negligence.

- Company leadership ignores emerging privacy regulations.

- The company is casual with third-party contracts to assign data privacy responsibility.

- The company has no method or process to track the company reputation online.

- The company pays no regards to the potential liability of technology wrongful acts by intentional or unintentional means.

- The company launches a new technology-enabled initiative or model without the appropriate testing and risk controls to protect for failure, misuse, or conflicts with laws and professional standards.

Unseen Liability

Any of the above can lead to a situation in which a company flirts with informational malpractice, an act that can lead to the injury, economic loss, or harm of another party.

Even the best doctors are insured against medical malpractice. No doctor would argue that his skills are so good or his intentions so positive that nothing could ever go badly enough to land him in court. The medical community recognizes this is a possibility and takes steps to protect itself from that liability. The technology community appears far less willing to consider unfortunate possibilities, yet the impacts of technology failures and abuses can be no less damaging and broad when it comes to a commercial loss or professional liability. In fact, one could argue that technology-related incidents - excluding bodily injury of course - have far greater potential for multi-party business liabilities as they potentially impact the thousands of people whose data is part of the web site, database, or server.

Companies across industries are deeply connected to the information world. They rely on the technological interdependence that pervades the global economy. From banks to retailers to hospitals to business services, technology has become indispensable, if not mission critical. Yet most companies are not insured for the possible downsides, the new unseen liabilities. The business insurance they do carry was never conceived and architected for the way technology has impacted the business world. Typical business insurance was developed, designed, priced and sold when a company's primary assets were hard goods and buildings and the potential disasters were floods and fire, slips and falls. *The truth is that current business insurance policies were written for a world that no longer exists.* That leaves modern companies involved in ever-growing forms of technology transformations, open to the prospect of negative consequences or unbudgeted crises and new-age liabilities.

Indeed, while company management may be slow to recognize the emerging liabilities created by technology, the legal industry is beginning to wake up, as evidenced by an increase in privacy class actions and IP lawsuits. I would assert that our economy is still a few years from more broadly defining technology dependence as both a business benefit *and* a responsibility. For the next few years, perhaps, we will identify the "ambulance chasers" of the information age as those cyber lawyers who argue what penalties, damages, and standards should define what constitutes information malpractice.

In 2010 the technology, legal, and insurance industries are on a crash course for professional turbulence, given the vacuum of historical legal precedent. Although the Internet is still in its infancy, the last fifteen years have taught us that technology's progress has outpaced our ability to

Unseen Liability

predict it—and govern it. Clearly, there is a lag in technology governance and accepted standards of care, and when there is a lag there is uncertainty. In support of this premise I was invited in 2009 to advise the World Economic Forum's council on the Future of the Internet. After two and a half days discussing the likely trajectory of the Internet and its future implications for business and society, we developed a position document for presentation later in Davos, 2010. The Future of the Internet findings were summarized in this later passage.

Future of the Internet 2010, World Economic Forum

Global Council Report, Dubai and Geneva, November 2009

Global Agenda Summit

Council Members

Jimmy Wales, CEO and Founder of Wikipedia

Jonathan Zittrain Professor of Law Harvard Law School

Ross Anderson University of Cambridge
Paul Twomey President and Chief Executive Officer (ICANN)
David L. Sifry CEO and Founder Technorati Inc.
Mitchell Baker Chairman and Founder Mozilla Corporation
Jonathan Hsu 24/7 CEO and Founder Real Media
Bruce Schneier Chief Security Technology Officer BT
Drew Bartkiewicz, VP Cyber Liability The Hartford
Jun Murai, Keio University
Ajit Jaokar, CEO FutureText
Alan Marcus, World Economic Forum
Dorothy Attwood, SVP AT&T Inc.
Wu Jianping Chairman CERNET

The Internet is a universal platform that not only drives innovation and creativity, but is also the major disruptive force in human affairs. It will therefore be central to any successful process of global redesign. Over the next five years we can expect:

- *Fast-paced change*
- *Rapid growth in the number of users online*
- *Rapid growth in application diversity*
- *Young people with new usage patterns and mindsets continuing to drive things*
- *Explosive growth in the online world – despite any recession*
- *There will be losers as well as winners – and the losers will be noisy*

The Internet's scope is expanding rapidly. We remarked in 2008 that it's not just the 1.3bn computer users but also the 2bn with mobile phones. And within 10 years most of the things connected to the Internet won't even be phones or PCs but other devices

Unseen Liability

from home appliances to control system sensors and actuators. The 'Internet policy' issue will affect more and more policy questions: not just privacy, but competition (because of network effects) and resilience (as replacing manual systems with socio-technical ones can give rise to new systemic risks).

Take for example the topical issue of cloud computing. This involves massive data aggregation and disintermediation; it raises questions of ownership, individual control, privacy, censorship, industrial organization and critical national infrastructure. Such a bundle of issues is difficult for traditional public policy to cope with.

Little wonder that policymakers ask, 'what should we do about the Internet?'

But the big problems arise simply because the Internet increasingly reflects the world. So when people talk about 'Internet policy' they may mean any of hundreds of policy issues: from the governance of the Internet's infrastructure; through the many complex socio-technical systems it supports – from email through Facebook to smart grids; industries that have been disrupted, such as the music industry; and cross-cutting issues such as privacy and online crime. In addition, business uncertainty remains a factor which forces world leaders to consider if appropriate risk transfer mechanisms are in place and sufficiently capitalized to absorb catastrophic impacts to the Internet as a "real time" business platform.

A fundamental tension is that while social policy problems have typically been tackled by national governments, the Internet is global – and has a history of self-governance on technical matters. The rate of technical change is simply too fast for legislation to keep up. There are also many sources of fragmentation, such as access, law, and censorship. Many of these stem from attempts at control, whether political, corporate or cultural.

So, what are the global collective-action problems? The principal ones are access (both to connectivity and to ideas), privacy, copyright, crime and dispute resolution. Each of these has a number of sub-problems; for example, privacy laws must deal with tussles between primary uses of data (e.g. medical records) and secondary uses (e.g. research).

Once this scope is understood, it should be clear that as Internet life increasingly touches on socio-technical issues, we will have to create multiple, issue-specific governance structures. But regulation without understanding the underlying principles is dangerous; an example is legislating to protect old business models based on copyright without understanding the new technical possibilities, let alone the usage practices and social setting of digital natives.

One area in which fresh collective action might be helpful is in ensuring openness and access to the Internet. Billions of (mostly poor) people do not have broadband but rely on mobile phones to get online; this is a great step forward for many, but the goal should be broadband – for access to the full richness of the Internet. Regulation must support a market for fixed and mobile network service provision that is competitive, has low barriers to entry, and can sustain growth.

Governments must also be careful not to overreact. A disruptive technology like the Internet can create losers as well as winners. If policy is driven by the losers, then society will also lose. Governments can mitigate the effects of disruption, but should not try to regulate to prevent it. Above all we need a collective commitment to keep the Internet open as the world's forum, social innovation platform and marketplace – universal, unfettered and end-to-end. Free trade in bits is just as critical for economic recovery, growth and progress as free trade in goods and services.

What's different about the Internet age is the magnitude of network effects; these can lead not just to rapid innovation on shared infrastructure, but to the dominance of large firms and to significantly increased complexity. When these factors operate on a global scale, unintended consequences become even more likely, and can lead to serious systemic risks.

The experience of the Internet community is that we need to involve everybody to manage these risks. We have managed to build the Internet to its current size by adopting an open and participatory approach with strong technical involvement and the participation of industry, civil society and government. Openness is essential for flexibility; the online world changes extremely quickly, so new stakeholders must be able to join the conversation quickly once they realize that they have a stake.

The challenge is finding a way to meld this approach with other governance mechanisms. This means designing multi-stakeholder structures for the institutions that deal with global problems with an online dimension – such as privacy, copyright, crime and dispute resolution. There, government will be one voice among many, and not always the final arbiter. And as ever more problems come to acquire an online dimension, the multi-stakeholder institution will become the default in international cooperation.

To sum up, systemic risk is best tackled by openness and collaboration, not centralizing and control.

Unseen Liability

Having returned from Dubai to finalize my thoughts for this book, it was clear to me that uncertainty may be part of the Internet future even more than I originally contemplated these last several years. Rather than businesses and professionals operating within a system of clear and understandable rules and regulations, information malpractice cases (even if not yet called that) are being argued individually (amazingly disconnected) by lawyers in a host of jurisdictions and courts. And although there is likely no alternative in the short term, this process of errors and omissions is a slow way to a system of technology governance and more predictable business principles, standards, and guidelines. Case law builds only as quickly as cases are decided. In fact, technology has advanced at a much faster pace than we even considered in 2000, thus leaving businesses in the crosshairs for liabilities they could never have seen coming.

Enlightened companies aware of the power of information technology now consider the scenario that their technology actions and decisions today may trigger an information malpractice incident tomorrow. That's true even if their current use of technology seems harmless. For example, what technologists may see as contextual marketing based on people's words in a personal email, Germans may view as surveillance. Both groups see the same use of technology's power but with very different user perceptions of what is legal, ethical, or appropriate; in other words, a blind spot. The "tail" of your technology neglect, arrogance, or abuse may be long as it lingers through cyberspace, passed around a growing multitude of servers.

With every step forward in our technology evolution new liabilities crop up, perhaps not immediately, but they can lurk like a lingering domino effect, residing as digital tidbits, electronic evidence, and Internet breadcrumbs across multiple servers, laptops, and storage devices. For highly regulated industries like banking and health care, there is a tremendous variety of what can go wrong when technology is leveraged and introduced in clumsy ways.

Consider for a moment the story of Comcast, a cable operator that was battling spotty public relations for perceived inadequate customer service and inaccessible employees. The problem was likely magnified, rightly or wrongly, by the tail of online social media and its expansive communications web. This perception of poor customer response grew as customers socialized that they could not get in touch with Comcast; instead they took their complaints out onto the Web. Forums and other public Internet spots filled with their chatter and the Comcast brand was a risk.

Unseen Liability

Enabled by new technology and a genuine interest to do good for his employer, a single Comcast engineer took it upon himself to set up a Twitter account and begin fielding questions and complaints from Comcast customers. This direct customer engagement was well received and highly trafficked by Comcast users. Comcast management was so pleased by the results that it handily empowered the entire engineering staff to go online to engage customers and solve their problems. The initiative, in fact, did not depend on the IT department or a capital expenditure for the purchase of additional IT assets. Utilization of the technology did not require a checkbook. Hooray for the lowered cost of technology, direct and personal exchanges with customers, in real time, fast and documented in cyberspace—forever!

How can this positive scenario of technology-enabled customer service possibly have a downside? Isn't it the goal of many Web 2.0 initiatives to be "authentic"? Initiative was taken, complaints were directly addressed, and of course costs were reduced (though new costs may have been created). What's the potential harm? What's the new risk? Technology empowerment is a double-edged sword. Good employees and good ideas are magnified and accessible, but so are bad ideas and potential "rogue" employees.

Incredible technology advancements for personal publishing, communication, and data sharing allow the Comcast engineers to more readily and intimately interact with customers. But these advancements don't automatically train individuals to conduct this Web-recorded interaction within specifically designed guidelines and/or established standards of care. Every employee communication via email or the Web is a voice of the company, a possible extension of its liability, even if conducted within an inherently "social" medium like Twitter or Facebook.

When is an engineer's professional advice or socialized idea a bad opinion? When is a bad opinion a recognized view of the company? And when does a questionable employee opinion become a public rant or slanderous comment about a competitor? Employee empowerment with the ability to publish so quickly and access increasingly sensitive data has also created the discomforting exposure of the rogue employee. Technology delivered via the Internet is a precise tool, a competitive weapon, or a blunt and self-destructing instrument depending on how wisely it is used and how thoughtfully it is introduced and monitored.

When a company like Comcast allows a decentralized, social, media-based customer service model, does it train its Internet foot soldiers to competently interact with customers without revealing confidential corporate information? Does the business train them in the discipline of refraining from making (publishing!) slanderous or critical comments about the competition, Comcast, or other customers? In fact, are the employees let loose to interact with customers with zero oversight, process, or training? The potential for positive business benefits is obvious, but so is the potential for less than desired outcomes and unintended consequences. Again, speed in the domain of Internet memory can kill when bad ideas from employees can have such a broad impact and seemingly infinite shelf life.

Whether an employee's intentions are good, impulsive, or malicious, the rogue employee has become a very real accelerant of information malpractice. As evidenced by insider data thefts, Internet rants, advertising lawsuits, personal injury claims, and massive IP infringements, the rogue employee is probably one of the greatest threats to companies today, and technology is a primary reason. Prior to such a transparent environment for data sharing and "free speech," the risk of a disgruntled or misguided employee was mitigated by physical, communication, and publishing limitations. Today, technology allows that employee a much larger stage, a bigger network, and a more public platform on which to disrupt or defame.

Fannie Mae learned this lesson when the Department of Justice discovered an ex–Fannie Mae employee had planted a virus in the company computers capable of wiping out the mortgage data of millions of American homeowners. The cost for business recovery and third-party liabilities would have been astronomical, with board-level implications for a lack of oversight. No doubt there was a time when that employee was a trusted individual, working with gained access and knowledge of Fannie Mae's technology. But when he changed his attitude toward his employer, his knowledge and technological acumen became powerful weapons of revenge against his firm.

Whose fault is it when an engineer insults a customer or an ex-employee trashes the company computer system? If the physical world is any indication, the ultimate blame may rest with the company, for its lack of technology mastery that made these unfortunate incidents possible. This is the dilemma of technology dependence: your technology, your problem. Perhaps risk managers would rather call it an accident, or ignorance, or even arrogance. But that will not likely buy a business or professional organization much sympathy in the courtroom, where twelve ordinary people will be asked to call it malpractice—of the information age kind.

In the world we live in, business must step up to the reality that it is largely unprepared (underinsured as well) for the new set of worst-case scenarios that can stem from technology and information. The terms

Unseen Liability

"data-driven" and "network dependent" will continue to have broader legal arguments and economic risk calculations associated with them. Disasters, mishaps, and abuses of the information age will not come in the form of a storm, flood, or fire. On the contrary, impacts and downstream liabilities from technology may be far more lasting. Unseen liabilities will involve information, and its impact will travel with frightening speed along the very technological pipes we so enjoy today. For every Internet and technological innovation we now embrace, there is a way it can be perverted, misused, abused, or just misunderstood.

Business understands traditional liabilities of the offline, physical world, but it has been slow to embrace the possibility that even bigger, more catastrophic liabilities exist on the virtual plane as well. No doctor goes into practice looking forward to the day he or she will be sued. But when and it if happens, that medical professional will have transferred the risk to an insurance backstop, a professional safety net. CIOs and CEOs alike should begin to ask if their company is protected against and prepared for a claim of information malpractice.

Chapter 5: The Other Side of New Media

There is so much media now with the Internet and people, and so easy and so cheap to start a newspaper or start a magazine, there's just millions of voices and people that want to be heard.

— Rupert Murdoch

New media has swept corporate America and the developed economies of the world. There is hardly a company on the globe that does not have a new media strategy or exposure. Even the stodgiest of old-line firms has embraced the social media concepts surrounding blogs, social networking, wikis, shareware, video uploads, and other variations on the new-media theme. Business has recognized the power new media has to connect buyers and sellers, to create communities in which marketing messages can be delivered, and to allow companies a glimpse into the minds of the consuming public. Business in every industry, and even professional industries like health care and law, has embraced new media as a critical strategy for growth and success in an increasingly social economy.

To be sure, new media has the potential to create significant dividends for business, but like any good thing, new media can also crush a company's reputation. New media and its widespread success have radically altered the responsibilities of companies *and their customers* in the marketplace of ideas, opinions, and ratings. Many companies I have analyzed that are using these new tools are playing by old rules, and this is leaving them open to trouble. This chapter will examine how new media has altered the landscape for business and permanently changed the rules, leaving companies responsible and liable for a host of activities they may never have imagined.

Like many new technologies, the early buzz around new media has been all about what great outcomes may occur. When marketers of 2010 gather around their conference tables to discuss creating a social network for customers or conducting a marketing push via Twitter, the focus is on how quickly, cheaply, and effectively the 2010 technology will enable this vision. In this paradigm of technology exuberance, going "viral" has only positive connotations, yet try to name any other use of the word where the connotation is not negative. What could be the downside of faster, cheaper, more personal contact with customers? It's easy to see why new media and communication technologies are so appealing.

What most companies have failed to perceive is that new media is more than a tool; it is a millennial shift in the media and communications paradigm. *What you say* about your goods and services is being trumped by *what others say* about your goods and services…and what others say can drown your own messaging in cyber seconds.

The commercial and legal world in which companies do business is altered by new media and, as a result, the role companies must play has shifted. Prior to Web 2.0, when companies communicated via traditional media like books, press releases, corporate brochures, static websites, and annual reports, the creators of this content understood their roles and responsibilities. They were in fact professionals, at least in training (editors, journalists, lawyers, communications experts, etc). They knew what was professionally expected of them as publishers of this content. They had training, guidelines, standards, peer checks, and experience.

In the new-media world, there is a different set of realities. Everyone—and I mean everyone—is a worldwide publisher, from an employee to a customer to a business partner, teenager, senior, fan, or critic. What we see being published by the millions of new participants, independent of the original intent of the writer, is often cast forever into the public domain: the worldwide Internet Dumpster and unofficial billboard all at the same time. Most companies, from my perspective, are unaware of or unprepared for this shift in media with business implications. As a result, they are leaving themselves exposed to potential problems.

From "Publisher" to "Monitor"

Consider the changes evident in content creation. In the first decade of the Internet, we called the assigned creators of content "publishers" or "content managers." They might have been traditional book publishers, but in general any company that created a document with printed text or branded on its website was taking on the responsibilities of a publisher and largely upholding the expected professional standards. As such, the company was responsible for the accuracy of the information; it was responsible for guarding against plagiarism and copyright infringement. Additionally, business lawyers analyzed the content for any potential misleading statements or potentially harmful, offensive, or slanderous information. Annual reports, marketing materials, press releases, and employee newsletters are all examples of thoughtful media, planned and reviewed.

This system of professional checks also extended to the creation of advertising. As a publisher in its own right, a business was legally responsible for its truthfulness and adherence to regulatory standards and industry-governed accepted general practices. By and large, the bulk of this content was centrally managed by the company and its representatives. It followed a well-regulated channel from concept to publishing. When a piece of content about the company was released on the world, company officials could be reasonably confident they had reviewed it and ensured it met all legal and ethical standards.

The unprecedented low cost and universal access of new media has rewritten the rules for traditional publishing and advertising, and for the liabilities of that content. Information about a company no longer travels via a carefully crafted and contained pipeline. Instead, by embracing new-media tools, companies have created multiple new ways for corporate content to be generated and displayed, often in real time, and often with little or no corporate oversight. For example, it is not uncommon for a firm to send its employees to a major trade show and instruct them to blog about what they see. How much review does that content go through before it hits the Internet? Company officials are lucky if the posts are spell-checked. The business demand for speed and the consumer demand for "authenticity" encourage employees to write fast and wide. A prolonged and orchestrated content review process would defeat the purpose of real-time communication, which is to create a sense of immediacy and connection with customers.

Here's another scenario. Companies eager to understand their consumers' sentiments have set up online forums encouraging visitors to post their comments and suggestions. They have also planted themselves in social media utilities to further listen to customer exchanges and provoke comments about a full range of topics that may or may not immediately relate to their brand. Although these techniques are a creative way to engage users of products and services, they can also be a way to be associated with or a "sponsor" of libel, slander, or defamation. Suppose a forum visitor blasts your competitor? Or suppose a visitor posts a rumor about an executive in your company, or with your competition? News travels fast online and it is also amazingly lasting. Suppose information posted by one of your forum visitors is read and reported by a news organization? Do you concur with the comment by leaving it untouched? Where does "official news" end and rumor begin? As with the previously discussed data privacy risk, the line of professional standards has been blurred, the rules made unclear, and the liabilities rendered uncertain.

In both of the aforementioned examples, a company may find itself grossly exposed, if not embarrassed, in this exploding world of new media and evolving standards. Blogs and forum posts might be considered company content, just like an ad or an annual report. But instead of having gone through a strict vetting process, the content has leapt directly onto the Internet. These scenarios illustrate how the mandate of the company has changed in the age of new media. The company cannot just consider itself a publisher of its own content. It

Unseen Liability

must now also be an active monitor of the content it is associated with; this includes content it creates, encourages, enables, or even sponsors. When word of mouth goes south, blame is issued and consequences ensue.

One of the key mandates in the new-media age is a new process surrounding content. In the old days, the company might have had a vetting process by which content went through a series of editors in-house and then perhaps to a legal or compliance officer for a check. Now the company needs new systems to monitor proliferating content generated via new media. It needs a process to ensure that content obeys laws and regulations and also societal norms governing the Internet. It needs new metrics to measure what is happening to content it produces (or is produced by others) and new technologies to help it understand how its content is being used and digested by the global community.

Clearly, a monitor and a publisher are not the same thing. Companies that have embraced new media also need to embrace their new responsibilities as thoughtful monitors, armed with the latest technologies for filtering, screening, and deleting content that can create liabilities on a global scale. Certainly, if something goes wrong—if a competitor loses business or an individual perceives that a company's content has caused harm—the brunt of that responsibility will be laid at a company's doorstep in a hurry. The public domain of the Internet is just that: *public*. Companies are increasingly liable for their abuse of the domain, the pollution of it, or the disregard for its well-being. Empowering customers and employees to directly add to a brand's content or a company's message can only increase liability for the company associated with it.

From "Brand Management" to "Reputation Management"

New media has also created unprecedented realities for the risks to company or professional reputation. In fact, I would say that reputation has never been in greater peril for business and individuals alike. For decades, the job of a brand manager was defined most by how well the message was controlled and how broadly it was received. Great companies—Procter & Gamble, Nike, Apple, and Wal-Mart—considered brand management a core element of their marketing model. All are firms that owe their success in part to careful, competent brand management. The care and feeding of a brand image, whether it's a B2C (business-to-consumer) or B2B (business-to-business) company, is what historically set great companies apart from the pack. One could refer to this previous generation of brand management as "static brand management" because few intermediaries could take your brand off message. You largely controlled the message, image, and feeling you wanted to create. With the

Unseen Liability

advent of new media, the role of brand managers has radically changed. Indeed, I would go so far as to say the title and responsibilities need a refresher. Reputation is at stake, and *reputation management* is redefining what brand management is all about.

Although most people believe that Web 1.0 was a major shift in business and wealth creation, the fundamental change was in commerce, not content. Web 2.0 is different: it is all about content. Several technological advancements have come along to radically change the makeup of the Internet. First, it became easier for individuals not only to generate websites themselves but also navigate across thousands of websites to opine, rank, rate, blog, upload, share, and, yes, gossip. Companies are no longer the only ones with voices online. In fact, the number of bloggers outnumbers the number of companies by multiples of one thousand. Furthermore, low-cost online tools have come onto the scene, empowering the masses to create even more content for the Web. There are now Web applications for communicating with the world that were once affordable only by large commercial enterprises. This is a game changer, and the result is a risk profile for business that will never be the same. Being liable or accountable for your own company message was one thing; being liable for the social and commercial intersection of your customers is another.

In response to this tsunami of opinion, ratings, and social graphs, my view is that companies need to shift their focus from brand management to reputation management and to consider reputation risks as part of their longer-term strategy. In today's new media world, the emphasis should not be on what *you* say about your brand, but how well you understand and respond to what *others* are saying about your brand and your competitors' brands. It's a job that of course requires speed, technology, and focus, but it also requires a greater understanding of the emerging laws and regulations that govern free speech, advertising, personal injury, defamation, and privacy. New-media realities require business leaders to consider their risk transfer possibilities when navigating this emerging environment of content proliferation and managing their risks online. Here are some basic suggestions for what reputation management means for Web 2.0 companies and professional organizations:

- A reputation manager must have antennas everywhere. It is not enough to know what is being said about your brand on your own site, or even on major consumer product ratings sites. What is being said about your brand in the vast universe of Web 2.0? On YouTube? On Facebook? On Twitter? On the millions of individual blogs that dot the blogosphere? That kind of monitoring requires both technology and processes to detect the issues and trends related to reputation sentiment.

- A reputation manager must move quickly. Damage to company and professional reputation can spread with the speed of two hands typing. Once detected, a reputation threat cannot be handled by forming a biweekly committee. A reputation crisis has to be addressed with the same speed at which it arrived. Traditional remedies like legal action and investigations may be far too slow to contain the damage to a brand's reputation. By the time you get a court date, the damage has been done.

- A reputation manager must engage with the online community. In the old days, brand and marketing managers might have faced their customers only on occasion, perhaps at an annual meeting or other carefully staged gathering. It was also possible for a company to brush off a rumor by refusing to comment on it via a traditional news outlet. In some cases, by ignoring it the issue went away with time. The tail was short because no Internet medium really allowed a tail to take shape. Not so in the new-media world. A brand manager might have been advised to ignore a rumor or reputation threat, but a reputation manager can't. A reputation manager has to get into the mix and engage with the critics and convey the company's message. Failure to do so only allows the critics to continue their reputation-harming behavior.

- A reputation manager must be adaptable. There is no one way to engage with new media. Once a reputation manager has finally settled on a strategy to communicate via one media, another one—faster and more popular—may emerge on the scene. The reputation manager must be willing to stay on top of social media developments and be ready to defend a reputation attack in whatever format it may take.

- Finally, a reputation manager must be aware that damage can pop up just about anywhere. It can come from a computer user in China who claims your product is made in factories rife with worker violations. Or it can come when your advertising agency's new viral ad campaign is a flop and spinning out of control through the customer community. Brand managers traveled in defined media circles. Reputation managers must cast wider nets of participation and responsibility.

An Era of Accountability

Unseen Liability

New media has the obvious potential to benefit customers and businesses in a variety of ways. One of the most significant is the way technology has ushered in an era of accountability. Go back for a moment to the scenario in which a company is accused of contracting with an overseas factory accused of abusing workers. In the period before Web 2.0, it might have been easy for a company to deny knowledge of the abuses. Indeed, in the old days of slower, less reliable communications technology, perhaps the information might really and truly never reached the appropriate ears at corporate headquarters.

New media alters that scenario because it makes it far less likely that the abuses in a factory will remain unreported or under the radar of traditional media. The amazing ability of *one person* armed with as little as a cell phone to create and distribute content on the World Wide Web means companies can be held to a greater level of accountability. Today, how can a company claim ignorance when any user could find the information with three clicks on a search engine? The opposite scenario, unfortunately, is equally possible: that a company's reputation is unfairly damaged by misinformation posted by a third party, be it a competing company or a malicious individual. Such misinformation not only has the potential to pollute public trust in the Internet's veracity but also creates longer-term liabilities for those businesses involved in the events of libel, slander, defamation, or advertising malpractice. Experience has shown me that the majority of companies are greatly underinsured for responding to or defending a new-media event or liability.

New media can, without hyperbole, be called a paradigm shift. As such, it should stand to reason that the old rules of content and brand management no longer apply. Companies must adjust to the reality of the new rules and change their processes, risk assumptions, and protections to be appropriately armed for marketing and messaging in the information age.

Chapter 6: Respecting the Internet Environment

The Realization that every digital movement is recorded and monitored itself will chill private behavior.

— Jonathan Zittrain

Most businesses I have underwritten for cyber risk initially believed they operated as some island of information and digital assets, protecting themselves from external perpetrators wishing them harm. Although this is true to a degree, it is also a very narrow concept of what the Internet means and is. If I reflect on my time in the technology sector and later insuring it, I have seen the Internet described as the following:

- a tactic
- a tool
- a technology
- a strategy
- an appliance
- a mechanism
- a channel
- a billboard
- a platform

- a service
- and most recently a compilation of cloud providers

These are common ways most businesspeople think about the Internet. They are not necessarily wrong; they are just grossly limiting how they view the significance of the Internet, the nervous system of the information age. One of the threats to the predictable and profitable functioning of the Internet is the idea that cyberspace is somehow a tool or novelty, an endeavor for IT folk or ADD-afflicted youths. It isn't. It's an environment unto itself—the principal domain of the information age, the space through which the new professional "slips and falls" and "pollution" will occur.

Seeing the Internet as an *environment* is more than just a semantic distinction.

- A tool is an object you personally wield; use it badly and you (or the few others in your proximity) might get hurt.
- An environment is a group experience, a public good, a global resource; misbehave and many may suffer the consequences. Like the physical environment of our earth, moves by one entity may cause unintended consequences to another.

Unseen Liability

When business fails to appreciate that the Internet is an environment, it puts the entire environment and all its inhabitants at risk. Indeed, that risk is already emerging. This is an electronic environment that literally and figuratively knows no borders, yet company brands, personal reputations, and individual privacy are accessible targets in ways the physical world cannot match. I spoke at a Web 2.0 conference in New York City on the topic of privacy in social media to a surprisingly passive audience and marginal attendance. Knowing my country's casual yet innovative approach to the Internet, I was not surprised.

I spoke one month later in Berlin on the same subject, and it was standing room only with an audience highly energized by the topic of privacy and technology advancement. Why the difference? One might surmise that national history gives Germans a different view of the Internet environment than it does Americans. What we may see as database marketing and contextual advertising, Germans may perceive as commercial—or governmental—surveillance. Commercial enterprises may deploy the same use of Internet technology but with very different cultural reactions to the potential for convenience and good, misuse and crimes.

What makes today's Internet an environment?

There are several ways the Internet differs from other communications tools that elevate it to the level of an environment, specifically the very public nature of its elements.

The Internet is a public medium, a global one in fact. The very name World Wide Web is front and center every time we view the browser letters "www." The Web is not owned or governed by any one entity or agency. Anyone can get on (in a free society of course), anyone can contribute, and anyone can use the medium for business or pleasure. Television, by comparison, is a medium owned and operated primarily by private companies, governed by public agencies, viewed by many but controlled by few. There were technological and economic reasons that yielded such a less than free environment for television.

The Internet provides public benefits. All the positive attributes of the Internet—speed, efficiency, convenience, communication, information—are benefits enjoyed by the public at large. In the eyes of an economist, the total resources of the Internet are a "common good," available to all yet vulnerable to those who would abuse it and lower its value to the commonality.

The Internet and our increasingly hungry participation in it grow primarily as a result of the collective trust we as a society put in it. We trust this revolutionary medium with our information, our news, our

Unseen Liability

personal and business communications, our shopping lists, credit cards, private journals, secrets, and family photos. Because we trust it, we continue to interact with it, and it thrives, grows, and evolves. It needs us and we need it, even though what "it" will be escapes our ability to predict. And herein lays the uncertainty for us all.

All these public elements and global citizenry involvement combine to create not a tool or a tactic, but an environment. The Internet is not just something we use; it's something we live in. For younger users it defines who they are, or at least who the world thinks they are through the lens of Web pages.

Why does that distinction matter?

If you bought a tool and used it with poor judgment, you might get hurt. You might even hurt the individuals in closest physical proximity. You might do some limited damage to a limited group, whether it was intentional or negligent. Say it's something silly like a power saw. You could cut yourself and perhaps another in the workshop with you. Say it's a larger tool, like a printing press. Misuse might result in an injured worker or maybe a lot of injured workers. But damage would likely stop at your property line and the walls of your factory, office, hospital, or cubicle. Catastrophic events are less likely.

If you operate a business or practice a professional in a more open, expanding, and interdependent environment and you act badly, the results ripple. When the Exxon *Valdez* hit an Alaskan reef and spilled 10 million gallons of crude oil into Prince William Sound, the impact was felt far beyond the walls of the energy company and the hull of the ship. Wildlife was harmed, livelihoods were impacted, millions in fines were levied, and individuals' reputations were put under harsh scrutiny. The company and even the very industry were tarnished for many years to come. As for the latent effects, all future companies hoping to conduct energy-related business in Alaska faced new hurdles, new questions, higher costs, and new barriers to their businesses. A mistake in the environment had a catastrophic impact as measured by the monetary, social, environmental, and reputation costs incurred. We just don't see the Internet the same way—yet.

What happens when a major company negatively impacts the Internet environment may be even more harmful, lasting, and profound than damage to the physical environment. Yet how many companies have environmental liability policies for the global and *interconnected* environment of the Internet? When a company fails to behave properly or is negligent in its electronic doings, the problem is not confined to its four walls and IT infrastructure. No, the viral impact for catastrophic events is that much greater.

Unseen Liability

Consider the impact of a major data breach, or "data spill," for lack of a better term. Like an oil spill, a data spill is an event of far-reaching consequences. A good example of this is retailer TJX (parent company of T.J. Maxx). In 2007, the company had a single, major data breach involving thousands of consumers—and the ripples are ongoing. The company itself was harmed; it suffered significant financial loss in fines and class action damages. And this publicly traded company also incurred the ongoing cost of proving to regulators it had fixed the problem and was on track for higher compliance standards. Harder to measure, TJX suffered the loss of its customers' confidence and damage to its reputation (a.k.a. stock price) in the marketplace. Because of ongoing class actions, the legal meter is still running.

But others were impacted by this "polluting" event as well; card issuance companies, suppliers that share data with TJX, and of course the consumers themselves who were now forced to deal with ID theft precautions, costs, and uncertainties. The consumers' personal data was *their* data until it became unceremoniously part of the public domain and spewed into the black market of personal data trading. Yet to the naked eye, the eye that does not understand how the Internet works, individuals barely raised an eyebrow of outrage or disdain until they started to notice the impact on their personal privacy several weeks later.

This highly publicized event weakened, if even for just a small segment of those affected, the public trust in the Internet. It weakened other companies' ability to do business online, since consumers became more hesitant and regulators more watchful. The harm moved outward from the original incident, like oil from a breached tanker, yet who really considered or even calculated the overall cost to the Internet environment? Some estimates for TJX alone put the costs up in excess of $250 million. But what about the cost to the Internet itself? Today, this quantification would be difficult if not impossible, but what is not hard to calculate is the total liability and operational expense one company can incur. And here is where most CIOs and CEOs have their heads in the sand of technology overconfidence.

A data spill is just one kind of environmental hazard on the Internet. Here are some others:

User IP infringement. If one person steals a copy of a movie, that's one loss to the studio. If one person steals a copy of a movie and distributes it online, the negative effects ripple throughout the movie distribution ecosystem, affecting the studio, the actors, the retailers, and the consumers. Any mass distribution of copyrighted material fits this bill. As Viacom and YouTube have discovered, it is very difficult to police IP infringement in the Web 2.0 Internet environment. When Viacom initially

Unseen Liability

complained to YouTube that its users were posting copyrighted material on its site, YouTube agreed to tell its users to take the offending material down.

But the Internet environment is too vast for that sort of one-to-one discipline. Wide public access and unmonitored terms of use means the bad actors can far outnumber the guardians. What's more, IP infringement does more than just damage the owner of any given piece of content. It creates problems throughout the ecosystem. New business models like YouTube or Twitter, predicated on the concept of massive user contribution, are threatened. Advertisers that might do business with YouTube and other user-generated content companies face challenges to their revenue streams. IP infringement does more than hurt the one or two companies involved; it pollutes the Internet environment and creates multiple unintended consequences. Such pollution makes it more difficult for businesses to have predictable outcomes and revenue streams, and even more difficult for Internet users to weigh the pros and cons of their online participation.

Reputation Blind Spots. In the days before Web 2.0, a rumor spread with the lethargic speed of speech. Today, rumor, gossip, and misinformation spread at the speed of mouse clicks. When a blogger posted a rumor that Apple CEO Steve Jobs had been taken from the company headquarters by ambulance, the "news" spread quickly affecting the stock and the reputations of Steve Jobs and Apple. Never mind that the rumor—I mean "Internet news"—wasn't true. When a search engine picked up a news story about United Airlines filing for bankruptcy, the stock tanked before the airline's press office was able to get the word out that the story was years old and the company's finances were just fine.

Accidents are not the only kind of reputation attacks that occur in the Internet environment. Some are intentional. Political rivals frequently tap the Internet to tarnish each other in hard-fought campaigns. Competitors leverage the anonymity of the Web to float misinformation about themselves or competitors, often via the social Web or blogosphere. Television on the other hand is more expensive and better regulated for truth and accuracy, especially because the costs to participate are multiple times higher for the average citizen.

We are truly at a turning point for frictionless, global communications. Just as data leaks and IP infringement create collateral damage, reputation attacks may have similar environmental effects. A growth in the number of these events can seriously undermine the trust placed by users in the Internet environment. Users start to wonder if the communications they are receiving are true, and businesses have to spend time dealing with tidal waves of misinformation. Little by little, more

Unseen Liability

thoughtful Internet citizens will start to worry if they should be participating in this forum, when it's clear that an individual or business reputation can be damaged in minutes on a global scale. As previously suggested, 2010 is still the infancy of the information age, so we are treading new waters when it comes to the governance of the world's most pivotal environment: The Internet. We can communicate with such breadth and speed that the unintended consequences for business and professionals are yet to be realized.

We have heard much about the Internet's "openness" and "connectivity" yet it is the business world's increasing interdependence that can have its downside. The pure technologists have a word for this phenomenon. It's called "interoperability." It is the state in which technology speaks the same language and allows businesses and individuals to interface with ease across time and space. Oceans, time zones, company walls: none of these are barriers anymore as information flows with automation and aggregation. Machines have the ability not only to eliminate the mundane tasks but also to be programmed to make decisions for us.

In the world of technologists, interoperability means efficiency and scale, but they often undervalue the reality that interoperability also means interdependency. One server going down in one location can set off a cascading domino effect within the company and out to its third-party supplier, customers, or partners that interact with the company. Other related businesses that depend on that server and data exchange are affected; companies or consumers depending on those interrupted companies can also feel the pain, and so on.

This is the biggest challenge for the advancement of cloud computing. As information flows, so flows business. As information stops, so stops business interaction. Clouds might not mean less security, but they most certainly can mean higher severity were an interruption to occur for multiple companies at once. As the world has witnessed with other major technology failures or professional omissions, vendors and customers of all the companies involved in a wide scale technology event can be impacted.

Such was the case with the Heartland payment systems event, which had a ripple effect on more than a hundred small banks and in excess of one million end customers. Although the company had purchased cyber liability insurance for their business, the amount of insurance was so small that it lasted only a few weeks into the process, which is still ongoing for defense, damages, and liabilities. In the environment of the Internet a local server can set off a regional, if not

Unseen Liability

global, event. Interoperability means we all share systems, in good times and in bad.

So, what must be done?

Given the environmental nature of the Internet, it stands to reason that business leaders must consider their technology risks and liabilities as they would their traditional exposures in the physical environment. Regulators and business leaders must craft more universal standards of care, reliable systems, rules, and regulations that make the Internet environment a predictable, sustainable place of business and personal interaction. The Internet world, like the physical and legal worlds, needs standards that promote the general public welfare of the environment. Businesses large and small must come to the understanding that an online injury, failure, or disaster to one is an injury to us all, as members of the same virtual ecosystem.

What will happen if we don't?

Sadly, that's not a theoretical question. Business already has a very grim case study of what happens when a new environment creates a "gold rush" attitude and nothing is done to protect the environment from harm.

Take a look at this list of attributes. You might think it is a description of our rapid investment technology and the Internet.

- Rapid growth in the sector

- Millions of new people in the environment
- Many new companies and spin-offs in the environment
- Transfer of risk to others who don't even know they assumed it
- Low barriers to entry
- Scant accountability
- Excessive valuations
- Self-governing

This in fact was the financial services industry in 2004–2008. It was a period of unprecedented growth in lending based on ever-widening standards for issuing credit. Millions of people who once sat on the financial sidelines dove in—as investors, as traders, as business owners, and as consumers. No one was reading the fine print—or the fine print was nowhere in site. New financial products and services like hedge funds, mortgage-backed securities, and online trading platforms gave rise to new businesses, and the new businesses spun off and created even more growth. The notion of transferring these abstract assets came into vogue, along with the easy money and lack of accountability that followed. Lenders packaged loans and resold them within a fluid environment; they

Unseen Liability

moved the financial risk along the pipeline, creating an interdependent and complex market from what were once contained transactions. There were very few barriers to entry, valuations on the companies involved soared sky high, and everyone embraced the notion that the free market was the best sort of governance. Regulators, such as they were, backed off or no longer even understood what they were regulating.

The resulting financial disaster should have been much easier to predict. A major credit crisis emerged as valuations of these nebulous assets hit reality, sending ripples throughout the financial services environment. With no one trusting the environment to ask for credit, give credit, or transfer credit, financial participation dried up. There was a broad and rapid "opt out" among the multi-stakeholders. Banks stopped lending, businesses faltered, bankruptcies rose, and investors fled the marketplace. Institutions that once looked like titans—Merrill Lynch, Bear Stearns, AIG—collapsed or teetered on the brink. Overconfidence was unmasked as a combination of arrogance and ignorance. No one new what the rules were, now that the rules were so poorly created and governed. Government stepped in to remedy the cause, save the financial environment, and bail out those impacted. The entire system is still being "rebuilt," at a higher cost to all.

It's not hard to see the parallels to today's largely ungoverned Internet. Like financial services, the Internet environment has seen a rapid growth. There are millions of new people participating in the space and unprecedented data collection by business, but few are considering the unintended consequences for technology errors, negligence, or abuse. Do we even consider the risks of data aggregation, automation, and access as we collectively accelerate our dependence—no, addiction—to more technology?

Professional and personal risk is being transferred in the expansive Web 2.0 environment at an even quicker pace as companies share their data, their networks, *and* their blind spots in digital joint ventures, online partnerships, and automated strategic alliances. Computer-to-computer interactions are increasing exponentially as companies extend their Web services, APIs, and real-time data transfers. Going into 2010, we are potentially all on autopilot and building our own mousetraps at the same time, with every data event we make and every data transaction business conducts.

So is the Internet environment on track for its own crisis, its own massive dilution of trust and confidence, and its own pile of legal arguments? Perhaps, but if the Internet is underinsured by business, or not insured at all, it will potentially be a very expensive crisis of trust that will usher the ugly words "bail out" to areas such as cloud computing, social media, and e-commerce in general. Participants in the environment—consumers, businesses, and bloggers—will react defensively to the perceived Internet insecurity, the vulnerability of the environment they trusted as much as the blue sky above them. They will start to pull back: pull back their content, their participation, their personal data, and their *trust*. Business would think twice about the efficiency gains of the Internet against the backdrop of systemic risk and an insecure platform.

Such actions would negatively impact the virtual environment in significant ways. If consumers won't share, marketers can't harvest knowledge. They can't create one-to-one advertising models with rich and current databases of personal information. Without advertising, the content options fade, as do many companies' business models. Without a willingness to share personal data, social networking and media sites falter. Banks and health-care industries slow productivity initiatives that conduct data transactions through APIs on the Internet; they get cautious, scared, and stop innovating.

Just as investors quickly pulled out of the financial market in 2008 and 2009, users can pull out of the Internet. Entrenched players or those totally dependent on information, networks, and servers—*especially those grossly underinsured*—will go belly up. The government will be forced to step in and help rebuild the environment with a new paradigm and set of burdens, at higher cost and at less efficiency than the free market. We will, in fact, have polluted the Internet ourselves and killed the goose that gave us all this golden egg.

It doesn't have to happen, of course. The credit crisis snuck up on us, but the trust crisis of the Internet has not yet taken hold. There are signs, however, that an inflection point about people's attitudes might be near. Users of social networking sites are starting to bristle at new data merchandising terms that put their privacy at risk. Marketers are hesitating to move ahead with behavioral-targeted advertising, especially in certain countries that may react negatively to the intrusion on personal privacy. The stakeholders and biggest users of the Internet environment are starting to show signs of concern and hesitation. Weekly incidents of data breaches or libel claims against good names are making established brands wary.

For so many reasons, both societal and economic, the Internet is in a pivotal year in 2010. If the Internet citizenry start to pull back in great numbers, the Internet version of the financial services implosion could be upon us. And like the financial services experience, the fallout will take most members of the ecosystem with it, not just the bad actors. The stock

Unseen Liability

values of information-rich companies will plummet as investors perceive information liabilities and technology vulnerabilities instead of growth and innovation.

The serious pollution or disruption of the Internet, as the backbone of the information age, is a risk to business and consumers alike. But its demise is not inevitable. Just as we were willing to face, and *insure for,* the uncertainties and risks of previous economic environments (agricultural age, industrial age, etc.), so too can we act to protect the expanding Internet environment, for both the public and private good.

Unseen Liability

Chapter 7: CIO Insurance—Hedging against Uncertainty

The first rule of any technology used in a business is that automation applied to an efficient operation will magnify the efficiency. The second is that automation applied to an inefficient operation will magnify the inefficiency.

— Bill Gates

Sometimes the bland subject of insurance does not evoke the same immediate attention as the subject of the Internet, especially to optimistic people who inherently and faithfully believe in the undeniable benefits of technology advancement. Business insurance, in particular, is the hallmark of the worst-case scenario. Often, that's the scenario no one wants to imagine or has had to imagine. And as the business importance and professional liability standards of CIOs grow, so grows the need for business insurance designed—no, *architected*—for the information age.

Most financially minded business leaders know that well-priced risk transfer (i.e., insurance) is a critical piece of an overall business model. CIOs do not purchase insurance because they think the business will fail. They buy insurance because there are just some things that can't be planned for, especially in the world of technology where the speed and breadth of use are trampling traditional paradigms, processes, and, yes, laws. Despite the young Internet's early lessons of disruption and unintended consequences, my experience suggests that less than one in ten CIOs have contemplated technology insurance or even know it exists. With the recent explosion of technology failures, abuses, and negligence (the seeds of information malpractice), the apparent denial of CIOs has continued to shock me. Information technology and the Internet are not just risks of uncertainty; they are also risks of business continuity on a global scale.

No business can operate on the premise that it has found a sure thing or that technology has buffered it from risk and business interruption. The world is an uncertain place. That's the reality, even for the optimists and believers that technology is somehow making the business world less random, less problematic, less variable. In fact, I believe that for the short term at least, it is quite the contrary. As we take into account how young the information age is we can look backward at the role of insurance in other major business movements and shifts in wealth creation.

Leaders in traditional industries (industrial, health, energy) purchase business insurance not because they are pessimistic but because

Unseen Liability

they recognize and respect the existence of uncertainty. Such a realization is occurring now in both the technology sector as well as the traditional sectors whose risk profile is directly linked to their mastery (or lack thereof) of technology. The graph below illustrates the two fundamental axes of information risk and information liability, which have become the axes of business and professional severity for virtually any company in any industry.

As it has in previous decades, business and professional insurance can play a critical role in supporting business growth and encouraging innovation. By providing their companies with a way to transfer risk and hedge against uncertainty, purchasers of business insurance are willing to take the chances and explore new technology frontiers that may benefit us all. Backed by the knowledge that their business is capitalized with insurance for the worst-case scenario, they have the freedom to chase the best-case scenario. Far from being a negative view, insurance is a primary reason for success and innovation, not just in the new-media world but in the physical world as well. Without being able to transfer or hedge against innovation risks, many of the marketplaces' great ideas would have gone untried for fear of failure or unintended consequences.

Today, however, the historically critical benefit provided by insurance is slipping in its effectiveness and applicability. For business, the nature and rate of uncertainty has changed as we have moved from human dependence to technology dependence, from personal liability to a self-service-model liability. The self-service world of person to machine, computer, or cell phone is comprised of data-driven and technology-dependent interaction. And for most industries, business insurance has not kept pace with the transformation.

Today, many businesses operate in a technology-dependent environment for which their insurance coverage is underpowered or misplaced. Traditional insurance policies were written for a world that communicated by telephone, stored customer information in a metal filing cabinet, and strictly controlled employee communication to the outside world. Person-to-person interactions dominated our industrial and professional service touch points. Thanks to the advancement of the Internet and its supporting information technologies, a business and social world like this no longer exists.

Still, few companies have made the necessary transformations to hedge against the uncertainty of the Internet and of operating their business within an increasing technology-empowered environment. Firms that would never consider lacking insurance coverage for fire, flood, professional malpractice, or discrimination are wide open to what could

Unseen Liability

go wrong in the information age. Their information risk profile has changed and most do not even know it.

This transition to the financial backstop of cyber risk and cyber insurance is more than just a philosophical shift for business and professionals; unseen (and uninsured) liabilities are a true threat to the continued success of business in the Internet environment. Indeed, the threat looms over the Internet itself should business ruin public trust in the medium. With business being unaware of these emerging technology risks and ignoring more strategic means to hedge against cyber uncertainty, the Internet success story may falter for all of us.

Just as insurance provided the critical risk transfer to support previous generations' growth and innovation, it must still be the building block in this new Internet environment. Technology alone cannot anticipate or prevent all the uncertainties, when technology itself is at the core of creating most of those uncertainties. Without a change in the mind-set of CIOs toward insurance, technology failures can torpedo an organization's growth and, worse yet, poison even a little bit more of public participation in the Internet's future. Perhaps a crafting of the real balance sheet for the information age would be help CIOs and CFOs align their view of an organization's newest set of assets and liabilities.

Business must face the reality of the inadequacy of traditional insurance and hold it up to the new demands of the Internet- and technology-enabled business environment.

Gaps of Traditional Insurance for Addressing Unseen Liabilities

Before businesses began widespread operations in the Internet- and technology-enabled environment, insurance focused on three core risks:

* Employee mistakes and professional liability; anything from discrimination in hiring practices to bad advice.

* Property insurance; hard asset loss; fire, flood, theft.

* General liability; a slip and fall on company premises, plus broad physical or commonsense claims against a business.

Technology has reconfigured all those elements and added new ones for which any company should seek to transfer risk. Let's look at the concept of employee error. Say it was a financial services professional recommending an investment strategy. Pre–Web 2.0, if an employee gave poor advice, chances are the only person harmed was the unfortunate customer on the receiving end. Today, given the ease of rapid global communication, such poor financial advice can spread like wildfire, impacting customers all over the world. The headache just got a lot bigger

Unseen Liability

and the potential severity of the liability that much broader. Welcome to the world of Internet-speed communications. Although these low-cost and open communications might be considered "frictionless," they are not without splinters of risk and unintended consequences.

Suppose it wasn't an innocent mistake or poor judgment but a bad actor in the company's midst. An employee behaved badly. Traditional insurance covers the traditional list of bad actions we imperfect human beings may commit while performing our professional service: discrimination, for example, or harassment. In the Internet environment, the bad actor running your server firewalls can do much more damage—much more.

A rogue employee can access sensitive databases and violate the privacy of your customers, reveal company secrets, damage careers and financial futures. Instead of impacting one person, one office, or even one division, this rogue player, the cyber player, has the power to impact many at once and with speed. Technology and the Internet itself give bad actors a much bigger weapon with which to do damage, create disruption, or spew misinformation. The openness of the Internet environment allows technology-emboldened bad actors to execute their damage on a global stage.

Asset loss is another area in which technology has completely rewritten the rules. Twenty years ago, a retailer's worst nightmare might have been to lose its inventory or sustain damages to its buildings with a fire, flood, or criminal acts. A company's most prized assets dating back to the early 1900s were largely tangible assets, easily captured within the accounting frameworks of professional accountants. The Internet and technology changed these valuations of company asserts; this was highlighted in the 2001 Brookings Institute's book, *Unseen Wealth*, which predicted a substantial shift in wealth-generating assets for the information age.

In fact, Wall Street began assigning new valuations based not on what a company *owned* in the physical world, but what a company *knew* via its growing information assets. Companies like Amazon.com and eBay, which owned little in the way of tangible assets, had created major data warehouses and IT infrastructures to tap into a deeper knowledge of their customers, enabling a data-rich platform for innovating new services at lower cost and greater scale. As a result, their company valuations soared. Today, these newer examples of Internet-centric companies are seen in the private and public valuations of companies like Google, Facebook, and Twitter.

Unseen Liability

With these lofty valuations of information and technology assets come new risks and business liabilities. If a company's data is its most prized asset, what happens when it's damaged or diluted? Stolen or lost? *Information* is an irreversibly growing commercial asset, but traditional insurance is still premised and priced based on what might happen if the warehouse burned down. Even though information is an asset that can't be seen, held, weighed, or measured (yet), it is the reason some companies succeed and others fail. The Internet environment helped business collect, transfer, and even store this commercially and socially prized new asset. The problem is that traditional insurance was written and modeled for a world that no longer exists.

General liability doesn't fit the bill.

This line of business insurance too has been disrupted by the Internet environment in terms of its relevancy and design. Companies once insured themselves against a slip and fall on the premises or a stolen bag or damaged vehicle. Although these physical scenarios are still possible, the Internet environment creates a new host of injuries to one that may quickly become an injury to many. Technology can do that: take a single action and multiply it exponentially to affect vast numbers of users.

This was never the intended purpose or original design of pricing models for traditional general liability (GL) insurance. Traditional GL insurance assumed a limited number of affected individuals. Certainly, underwriters and actuaries of GL policies over the last fifty years never envisioned or quantified the issues of scale and severity possible through the use of cloud networks and Web 2.0 technologies, which have eliminated global boundaries. Technology has enabled uncertainty and systemic risk to creep out from behind traditional insurance protections and threaten companies in new ways.

As these exposures are both created by *and* magnified by the Internet environment, so too is the economic impact of any one of them. A rogue employee leaks the data of millions of customers. A network outage interrupts your business or, worse yet, your customer's business. Interoperability cuts both ways: it can expand everyone's success as well as everyone's pain. Because technology connects so many businesses and customers, any negative event happens not to the few but to the many. This phenomenon greatly raises the cost of a cleanup. If your employee hurts one individual, the payout is limited. If the employee hurts millions, the math follows suit. Thanks to the Internet environment, the economics of success are far beyond what businesses might have imagined a decade ago. That's true for the economics of a failure too. In the open

Unseen Liability

environment of Web 2.0, it appears that anything and everything can happen globally.

Given the new era of the Internet environment, what should business be insured for? And why will cyber insurance need to operate differently than traditional insurance?

Operational risks. What do these look like? Here are some examples:

Direct costs. These are the expenses a company could incur in the event of a technology incident. For instance, the company could be insured for a business interruption if the network goes out. A company should be insured for the cost of notifying people in the event of a data privacy incident and also for the cyber investigation costs of looking for that data breach. These are costs traditional insurance may not have imagined.

Reputation risk. We have already examined how reputation damage can occur with lightning speed in an Internet environment. This is the insurance that would cover the cost of those events. What kind of reputation events could cost you money? Many. Examples: a drop in your stock price (the result of misinformation or old information) or a rumor about your company or its officers. Cyber insurance would cover the cost of a public relations firm to rebuild your reputation or to hire a lawyer or to set up a call center to field customer questions and concerns.

Regulatory risk. The regulatory issues surrounding the Internet are in constant flux. What you do today, which may be perfectly within current accepted standards, could be ruled out of bounds down the road as regulator standards evolve. Insurance could cover the cost of bringing your business into compliance with new regulations as well as the cost of penalties and fees.

Also, as companies do business globally, companies may seek to transfer the risk of running into different rules, standards, and laws in different countries. In the United States, what one business may call behavioral advertising may be considered surveillance by European regulators. Companies need to be prepared for differences among cultures and countries as the Internet becomes a business, social, and civic platform. This is another example of how insurance allows companies to grow and explore new markets, even virtual and digital markets.

Without the protection of insurance, would a company risk venturing into new markets? Would a firm delay or decline to take its business model to Europe? To Asia? Would regulatory and cultural risks be too uncertain a proposition to be worthwhile? The value of insurance in the Internet environment has never been clearer. Without the ability to

Unseen Liability

transfer risk, companies may simply seek to avoid it, derailing the global opportunities afforded by the technology.

Professional and Business Liability

There is great uncertainty surrounding the potential liability of technology and Internet wrongful acts by companies and their employees. The liability damage of information malpractice, therefore, is the wild card as most laws, regulations, business norms, and accepted practices have not kept pace with technology advancement.

Operational expenses can be quantified and estimated fairly accurately. A company can establish a base understanding of how exposed it may be by looking at available data: how many customers, how many hours of credit monitoring, how high is the fee or penalty, etc.? These things may be troublesome, but they can be counted based on regulations and previous incidents, especially for privacy and security incidents. Similarly, a company can calculate the cost of a cyber investigation. But liability is the great unknown.

How much would it cost for a company to defend itself if it were accused of information malpractice? It's very difficult to calculate because so many factors can come into play, given the relative newness of the Internet and our ability to communicate so rapidly and freely. What would be the nature of the malpractice? How personal was the leaked data? How vast was the IP infringement committed? Was it an intentional act or an accident? What was the technology oversight and management awareness? What ultimately is the standard of care to make profits with other people's information? What is the standard of care to operate wisely in the social Web? These are wild cards. They are the unseen liabilities. The operational expenses may be quantified, but the liabilities are yet to be determined.

Why don't businesses have this coverage already?

If it's true that technology has created so much uncertainty, why are businesses still operating without more explicit and meaningful technology risk insurance? Where is the insurance coverage for the brave new world we find ourselves in today? What is holding up the evolution of the industry to deal with these new business risks and these unseen liabilities?

The answer is threefold:

Lack of product innovation for real cyber insurance.

Insurance companies have been slow to generate the products necessary to meet the various forms of technology risk and information liabilities. Most insurance still follows the traditional models, creating protection mainly for hard assets and human errors, with rating models calculating damages limited to just a handful of individuals.

Unseen Liability

In the Internet environment, limits are erased and the potential impact ripples downstream to many others. The loss of customer files in a fire in the company headquarters is not the same thing as a loss of customer files resulting from a data breach. In the fire, the event is over when the smoke clears. In the data breach, the fire may spread far beyond the reaches of the initially impacted company and rage unchecked for quite some time. The tail of the event is potentially years, not months. As business awareness grows there will likely be a spurt in innovative cyber insurance products designed to address the technological realities of the ever-changing Internet environment.

Lack of broker education. Insurance brokers are used to selling traditional products for traditional problems and risks. Brokers need to be better educated in the fundamental changes that have taken place thanks to the advent of the Internet environment and the role insurance must play in light of these new risks. When I first spoke of "information malpractice" at the broker convention in Chicago, it was clear to me that this was the first time anyone in the room had heard the phrase or even considered the concept in concrete terms. Individually they may have sensed that a change was occurring in their industry, but they were not seeking the necessary information to truly embrace that change and understand it in the context of their own actions and mandate. In many cases, it will be a broker who first brings this information to business owners.

The brokers must be the front lines of this evolution. They are the messengers of both the changes in the environment and the changes in the products necessary to manage in the new reality. This requires a different mind-set, and even skill set, within the profession of insurance brokers. They need to understand technology's impact and direction as much as technologists do. They need to understand the legal implications of technology's progress as much as lawyers do. They need to acknowledge the existence of technology uncertainty as much as underwriters do. And, lastly, they need to understand the business liabilities and risks as much as CFOs and CIOs do. Brokers have the potential to herald a new era of business insurance, a more responsive and dynamic one, for their customers and their industry.

Companies' lack of awareness. Quite frankly, if business owners were demanding insurance products to hedge against technology risk, the marketplace would be awash in both products and sellers. However, many corporate leaders are failing to see this as a priority. Some are ignorant; they do not see the risks they are facing. They don't understand how quickly interoperability binds them to other businesses and business laws around the world. They don't see that their best assets

Unseen Liability

are no longer physical, but intellectual, digital, and fluid. Others perhaps are arrogant and believe their company's mastery of technology is "ahead of the curve" and above reproach. They believe the *intent* of their technology advancement is so positive, the downside will never happen. This is the optimism of the technology-inspired business, for better or worse. Clinging to this narrow vision often results in a technology blind spot, with disastrous consequences

Here's one more reason business should act now to address the new needs of insurance in the Internet environment: the cost of transferring this risk is advantageously low. Given the fact that insurance for the Internet environment is in its earliest stages, this is potentially the least expensive that cyber insurance will ever be, at least until the full economic impacts of unseen liabilities are realized.

Clearly, the risk associated with technology in business is not going away. In fact, it is accelerating. Indeed, as technology capabilities expand and more companies find broader ways to use information, the marriage between business and technology will only become more tightly bound. Given the current trajectory of technology-created incidents, more companies will experience the economic consequences of data breaches, IP infringements, rogue employees, Internet liabilities, and other forms of information malpractice. The prediction is that these incidents will fuel the market for this new type of insurance coverage. It is a product category on the cusp of a boom.

Does my company need it?

Let's put it this way. The need for cyber insurance is directly proportional to the degree that a business's professional services, delivery of products, reputation, and profits depend on the accurate and available use of technology. The more a business depends on technology, the more its business partners depend on it, thereby raising the mantle of risk to quite high levels of severity. In fact, the following formula is just one representative look at how one could consider the *orders of magnitude* for a company's cyber risk and unseen liabilities.

$$\text{Cyber Risk Factor} = \int \frac{\$ \text{ value of data} + \$ \text{ liability of data} + \$ \text{ value of brand} + \$ \text{ annual revenues}}{1/\text{no. of servers} + 1/\text{no. of employees} + 1/\text{no. of websites} + 1/\text{no. of customers}}$$

Of course, a business increases its cyber risk factor as any one of the inputs is increased year after year. Although this is a formula to demonstrate critical factors, actual technology risk underwriters look at additional factors that pose the following types of questions to companies looking to mitigate their exposures to unseen liabilities.

Are you collecting more data than you need?

Unseen Liability

The cost of data storage is so low that many companies fail to police themselves when it comes to data collection. Marketing experts tell us that collecting data is good and so companies do it, even though they may have no real use for the data. This is an unnecessary risk. The data you collect may be useless to your company, but someone else might find it very valuable, perhaps valuable enough to buy it from you. Or steal it from you. In either case, the individuals involved might well complain that you did not carefully safeguard their data. From your perspective, it may not have been worth safeguarding. But if your belief is not universally held, you open yourself to risk by touching this data at all. Don't collect data you don't need; it only opens you to liability regarding its safe handling.

Are you collecting reputation data?

Consider the kind of data you are collecting and what it could be used for. Is this data that could hurt a reputation if it were to leak or be delivered to third parties? You may be collecting it for your own reasons, but if it could be leveraged to alter a reputation, it has a new set of values. Consider whether having that data is worth the cost of protecting it. If it is necessary to your business, have you set the appropriate safeguards? Have you hedged against the risk? Are you ready for the worst-case scenario?

Are you collecting regulated data?

This data is information government agencies may have interest in. As a result, you might need to set aside a budget to communicate effectively with regulators about this data. Remember that regulators pertain not just to the governing bodies of your home base, but to any jurisdiction in which you may do business. Although your home country may okay the collection of certain data, the same regulations may not apply in China. New York may allow the retention of personal data; California may have other plans. Since regulation in the Internet environment is patchwork rather than centrally coordinated, understanding what regulated data you need and why is essential.

Are you enforcing your terms of use?

It's not enough to have rules on your books; you need to show you are enforcing them. Viacom's dispute with YouTube revolved around this issue. Viacom complained that YouTube users were posting copyrighted content on the YouTube site. YouTube responded that its terms of use forbid this. Viacom demanded YouTube walk its talk and enforce those rules. This is not something YouTube has found easy or cheap to achieve. Your terms of use are your marching orders. Are you prepared to execute on the standards you have set? Further, are you documenting your efforts to maintain and enforce your standards? Could

Unseen Liability

you produce proof of this if asked? There could come a time when you will need to show that your company was not asleep at the switch, but an active guardian of the Internet environment.

Are you monitoring the latest privacy laws?

Data privacy is a topic in constant flux. Companies must be vigilant for changes in the regulatory environment and also in the cultural norms and standards surrounding privacy. What can a customer expect from you in terms of privacy protection? What is your liability if there is a privacy breach? You need to understand these issues up front, not as they unfold in the midst of a crisis. Furthermore, revisit your privacy regulations early and often. The speed with which laws and even social norms change is lightening fast. This is not a set-it-and-forget-it element of your business. It requires ongoing attention and refreshing.

Are you tracking new advertising laws?

This ties in to privacy issues and is an area in which the arrogance-ignorance factor can be quite high. In the advertising and marketing silos of a company, everything is about the upside. The advent of a new idea for advertising and marketing will be met with cheers rather than skepticism. The advertising industry, like the technology industry, attracts optimists. It is therefore critical for a company to carefully monitor the rules and regulations surrounding advertising to be sure that the next "great idea" is not a setup for a day in court.

Following are additional questions to ask when assessing technology exposures:

- Does your network directly support delivery of your goods or services?
- Does your website encourage customers to self-service their transactions, interactions, etc?
- Do third-party businesses depend on your network availability?
- Do you have company confidential data in your networks? Laptops?
- The list continues . . .

The risks of the Internet environment are real and growing exponentially as new technologies and new ways of using them in a business setting come online. Companies can no longer rely on old business strategies. Nor can they rely on traditional insurance policies to protect them. Just as a wise company looks ahead to the next great technological evolution, it must also hedge against the uncertainty of that evolution. Companies must step up and demand insurance protection

Unseen Liability

specific to the business risks and liabilities of the information age. The insurance industry must step up with innovative products and appropriate education for those who will promote those products out to customers. The risk of information malpractice is real.

The responsibility of any company or professional active in the cyber environment is to be proactive and transfer that risk appropriately, not just for their own sake but for the sake of the public trust in the Internet. Using other previous business revolutions as examples, the professional move to insure technology uncertainty—*and the corresponding unseen liabilities*—will free businesses to innovate further while keeping the interests of their brand, their customers, and their partners safe.

Unseen Liability

Chapter 8: Information Malpractice in Every Industry

The most exciting breakthroughs of the twenty-first century will not occur because of technology but because of an expanding concept of what it means to be human.
— John Naisbitt

The one reality most apparent over the last few years is that technology-related incidents have struck virtually every industry and every professional services sector. Few people, however, have connected the dots of these incidents to recognize that they have been created by, related to, or exacerbated by the presence of technology in our world. Data drives business, servers support transactions, and computers provide a baseline for services ranging from health care to banking to law. The Internet is the looking glass into these complex transactions, data calls, and network exchanges.

Looking ahead, no industry will be able to stand apart and safely assume it is free of the unseen liability of technology. At this juncture, technology is too well embedded in every aspect of business for any industry to routinely operate outside its confines. Even the least technological businesses use email, computers and have Internet access. Even the most Stone Age of industries has embraced the basic tenants of data storage and search-engine marketing. Technology has made its presence felt in every area of the marketplace, probably more so over than last decade than any other previous time. We can acknowledge, however, that some industries made investments in technology dependence at a faster pace.

That said, not all industries will be affected in the same way or at the same time. Each industry has its own set of unique characteristics and relationship with technology; therefore, there is no one-size-fits-all response to the problem of unseen liability. Different industries will experience the problem with varying degrees of exposure and readiness. The key for any business is to better understand its unique industry's exposure to technology, and the necessary response. No industry can afford to stand still and wait for the inevitable. In fact, the potential for technology errors is growing not just by the *number* of scenarios possible but by the *severity* of risk and liabilities, given the market movement to cloud computing, social media, and Internet dependence.

In this chapter, I'll suggest some of the primary industries most affected by the new risks of technology. Although by no means in a sufficient degree of detail, I'll show how each industry is exposed, the position it's in right now, and its mandate for future behavior.

Retail

One of the early adopters of the online marketplace, the retail industry is further along the path of technology dependence, both in benefiting from technology and experiencing its downside. During Web 1.0 of the late 1990s, the Internet delivered retailers the potential for a more global marketplace. At the same time, massive data aggregation created pitfalls never imagined in pre-Internet days. As retailers, marketers, and advertisers continue to build their growth platforms on emerging Web 2.0 technologies, they will also have to face the new risks seeded throughout their industry. Already, the strain is starting to show.

Exposure: One-to-one marketing was the process that allowed retail to boom over the last decade. The multi-tenant databases of personal data quickly matched people with specific "personalized" products and services. But even as information gathering made retailers and marketers smarter and more targeted in their efforts, the one-to-one practices also created unseen liabilities. All that data leveraged for targeted marketing campaigns can also be leveraged for other uses—such as ID theft. Retailers and their partners have become prime targets for hackers, since their databases are full of personally identifying information. Their data warehouses of consumer information are also enormous concentrations of risk when it comes to protecting tremendous volumes of *regulated*, personally identifiable information. Did I use the word "regulated?" Yes, I did. Data regulation has crept into retailers' risk profiles, which means they have mounting legal liabilities, and not just with their customers. They are facing potential operational risks to comply with an ever-growing set of US and international regulations that govern how personal data is collected, stored, protected, and legally shared.

Status: Instances of data breaches in the retail arena are mounting. In 2007, TJX, the parent company of T.J. Maxx and other retailers, dropped a bombshell by announcing that more than 45 million credit and debit card numbers had been stolen from its IT systems. The company said it had taken some measures over the previous years to protect customer data through obfuscation and encryption. But TJX didn't apply these policies uniformly across its IT systems; as a result, it could not say for sure what was the extent of the damage caused by the data breach. A centralized strategy for data protection did not match with a decentralized management of that strategy. Just as noteworthy, a lack of risk transfer analysis for information malpractice led TJX to several hundred millions of dollars of uninsured costs, damages, expenses, and fines. This was a technology incident that quickly elevated to board-level concerns, national attention, and stock-dropping news.

Two years later, Heartland Payment Systems, a credit card processing company servicing retailers, went public with the fact that their network had been breached and unauthorized access gained to the credit card transactions it handled. How many credit card records were compromised? News reports suggest more than 50 million names and

Unseen Liability

counting, with claims for damages limited not only to consumers but also the businesses negatively impacted by the Heartland incident. Technology errors and omissions can create B2B liabilities as quickly as they create them for B2C scenarios.

Both these instances received significant press coverage and noise in the consumer community, especially during the initial wave of customer concern and uncertainty. Some online consumers began to question, is it safe to shop online? Who has my data and why? Am I now likely to be a victim of fraud? Am I better off spending my money in the brick-and-mortar world and not risking the insecure online environment? (This one is a fallacy, as even brick-and-mortar systems are now computerized point-of-sale systems that operate back into the same major data centers as the online systems.)

These are the dynamics that can undermine the trust of a digital economy, the Internet environment. For a company that experienced the breach, these are the forces that can place them at the bull's-eye of an angry mob, a litigious class action, or a punishing government agency. If broad consumer trust is breached and people's personal data assets are compromised, consumers pull back and the ability of the e-commerce business to thrive is jeopardized.

Mandate: Retail must move swiftly to reestablish and protect trust. Consumers are already experiencing doubts in the wake of the highly publicized data breaches, and that rift will only grow. Two suggested actions are to (1) insure for data assets and liabilities the same way your company insures for financial and physical assets and liabilities and (2) be more transparent about how your company is using someone's personal data for transactions, matching, services, and advertising. Below is one such emerging practice.

Transparent Personalization. Consumers should have a better idea of what is happening to their data behind the scenes. Wal-Mart has taken a first step toward this process by adding a button (more like a soft disclaimer) to its online ads. When a visitor to a Wal-Mart site sees an ad, there may also be a button to click for more information—information that may explain to the customer why he or she is receiving that particular ad. In fact, there are at least seven reasons, or triggers, that explain why the ad or site is performing as it is. This one-to-one transparency helps customers feel more like they're working in partnership with their retailers and less like they're under hidden surveillance. They can even opt out of certain ad types, which gives them an even greater sense of control, if not security. This improved consumer trust will be critical to the ongoing functioning of the e-commerce community. In contrast, if individuals start to assume retailers are being lax with their data, or simply leveraging it for

Unseen Liability

their own greedy purposes, that data valve will shut off and shoppers will go back to brick-and-mortar options.

Health Care

Health care has the moderate advantage of having been slow to fully leverage technology-enabled services and Internet interactions for marketing, servicing, and caring. Such a lag in the industry's technology adoption provides the health-care sector with the 20/20 vision benefit of learning from other industries and parsing out the best practices from among them. But perhaps this suggestion is just a minor advantage, since health care has its own burdens when it comes to technology risk related to people's health and reputations.

For example, an individual might be mildly annoyed to see his Amazon shopping list leaked onto the Internet, or know that his credit card needs to be cancelled, renewed, and monitored for a period of time. This is more of a nuisance than a real threat to his reputation. However, he is going to have a far more emotional reaction if his electronic medical history were to follow that path of improper public dissemination. And yet the health-care sector is now moving at a blistering pace toward the broad use of EMRs (electronic medical records). In fact, financial and political pressures are growing to make every facet of health care more dependent on the faster, leaner, and more efficient technology solutions.

Like retail, personal data will become the lifeblood of the system, of the environment, of the risks. Health care should, in fact, grow into the information age for reasons of better care and financial practicality, but the risk of consumer-driven, technology-dependent health care is significant and should not be overlooked.

Exposure: Under pressure to reduce costs and streamline delivery of services, health care is being asked to turn to technology for everything from electronic record keeping to online health education and training. Doctors are using computers in the examining room to aid and speed diagnosis. Back offices are using technology to track payments and manage records. Consumers are increasingly turning to the Internet for health information and guidance, or to connect with communities for the sharing of experiences and ratings of doctors and medications. Ready or not, economic necessity has thrust health care into the technological minefield.

Status: The risks and liabilities of the Internet age are already impacting health care. Certainly, the data-breach risks experienced by retailers are also an issue for health care. But in the health care arena, a data accident doesn't have to happen on a wide scale to be a big headache. Consider the experience of Brittney Spears, the very public pop star whose tabloid-chronicled emotional breakdown created an unseen liability

Unseen Liability

for the UCLA Medical Center. Ms. Spears was at one point hospitalized at the UCLA facility. Interest in her story was high and several weeks after she was released, information about her stay made its way into the public arena. There was data about her diagnosis, her medications, and her doctor. A rogue employee of the hospital made the information public. The information was currency and a UCLA staffer was clearly willing to traffic in it. Her privacy was jeopardized and liability was unveiled.

It was an incident involving just one individual, but the ripple effects were significant. Certainly, Ms. Spears's reputation was compromised; would an entertainment company now hire her at the same monetary terms, knowing the details of her medical woes? Would her ability to earn a living as a performer be threatened? What about the other companies dependent upon Ms. Spears's popularity—sponsors or movie studios or the members of her backup band? Their ability to earn could also be damaged. The rogue employee at the UCLA Medical Center has opened up a large swath of unseen liability for the hospital. Technology risk in this case was not related to how many people were affected. Damage can be just as expensive when just one person is at the core of an incident of information malpractice.

The mandate: Risk managers in health care should follow and consider the benefits of risk transfer for technology errors in the same way they insure human errors (a.k.a. medical malpractice). Of all the industries, health care should be the quickest to understand how risk and liability are a fact of professional life. Error is not erased by the advent of technology. Instead, new kinds of errors emerge and technology allows them to happen on a more global scale. Just as health care has taken steps to address the risk of human error, it must now address the new risks created by the digital environment.

Banking

The impact of unseen liability on the banking industry is already playing out in full swing, as we witnessed in the recent credit crisis. Much of the upheaval can be traced to what technology allowed the financial services industry to do, but did not make it prepare for. There was a downside to the financial services boom: thanks to technology, bad business decisions were made faster through reliance on more and more software automation. Mortgages, loans, and faceless credit applications were approved not at the hands of a thoughtful underwriter, but by a preprogrammed online application whose algorithms ran wild and unchecked. Data collection *and* data automation have given rise to new and accelerating financial business liabilities, creating the next wave of professional blind spots.

Unseen Liability

Exposure: As in the sectors of retail and health care, the banking industry began its exposure to new risk when it started aggregating ever-greater volumes on its customers. Decades ago, banks were primarily local institutions. Relationships with customers were quite literally one to one. A banker knew his customers from cradle to grave and kept their records in a filing cabinet in his office. The advent of technology allowed financial services institutions to grow from local banks to global behemoths. Paper records became a quaint memory as financial giants were able to collect and store the data of millions. That data created a treasure trove of personal information—and a wide swath of liability for not judiciously using and protecting it.

As is the case with health care, financial data is highly personal and sensitive. A breach of this information in 2009 became a dramatic occurrence, a stock-dropping event, and a painful company liability. The more banks collected, the more they exposed themselves to the risk of an inadvertent data spill or a well-orchestrated data heist. With most customer interactions now moving online and onto ATM kiosks, financial services are evolving from a traditional professional liability risk (human error) to a self-service model that is clearly a technology liability and risk.

Looking for speed, efficiency, and a data-driven model for self-service, financial services embraced technological advances such as online banking, Internet stock trading, and financial education websites complete with mortgage calculators and retirement advice. All these elements attracted consumers in droves. But they also opened the banks to a new level of risk. If a human bank employee gives a customer bad advice, that human employee has committed a professional error: financial advisor "malpractice." What happens when the advice comes from an avatar, a software model, or database algorithm? Who is responsible then? Technology has opened avenues of risk *It's a Wonderful Life*'s George Bailey could never have imagined. Technology has become a critical engine in the financial services boom. With that expansion comes the expanded risk.

Status: As the credit crunch deepens, the question as to what role technology played in the financial collapse is being asked. Were consumers able to self-serve online when they should have had better human advice? Did technology platforms allow a crisis in confidence to spread further and faster than it might have in pre–Web 2.0 days? How much of the pain we are now experiencing is related to the technology blind spots of the financial services industry? Have bankers hedged against that risk? And in the wake of massive data spills at Bank of America, Heartland Payment Systems, and Citigroup are we also seeing the downside of major data aggregation?

Unseen Liability

Mandate: Technology fueled a massive financial boom. Now it has ushered in a bust where both credit and trust in data privacy have dried up. Going forward, financial services firms need to ask themselves what they are doing with data. Are they collecting more than they need? Are they enforcing their own terms of service? Are they monitoring for the latest privacy laws? Are they automating decisions too much, too fast? And what steps have these companies taken to insure themselves in this new world of data currency and information malpractice? Clearly for the financial services sector, traditional insurance was written for world that no longer exists.

Technology Providers

One reality about technology risk is that technology providers have become the platform to move our economy and redefine business liability, all in the same decade. The technology sector hasn't just created unseen liability for other businesses; the industry has created plenty of its own to deal with. Of all industries in the marketplace, none has manifested more of a blind spot for technology risk than the technology makers and providers themselves. Eternal optimists (and I loved being one myself), they continued to chase the next big thing. The answer to any new problem actually created by technology was—ironically, but not surprisingly—more, better technology. Processing power, software, and bandwidth have led us all into a world where communication moves at lighting speed, information is widely available rather than restricted, and economic possibilities are expanded for all. That's the good news. Now, along with other industries, technology is facing its hangover and its reality check of self-governance and sustainability.

Exposure: The honeymoon for blank-check, knee-jerk technology spending probably ended around 2001, when corporate executives began demanding evidence that their IT budgets were buying something of value and "ROI" became a necessity to justify future IT investment. That first blast of cold air was followed by continued scrutiny of technology: how it works, how it should work, and now in this world so intertwined with technology, how it *must* work. Technology providers are exposed to unseen liability as their customers begin to recognize just how great the catastrophe would be if the technology were to fail.

Information technology itself has gone from a necessary evil in the 1990s to a mission-critical function in virtually every line of business. Industries across the spectrum have begun to hold their technology suppliers more accountable for glitches, outages, service interruptions, and failures. "The server is down" or "the software crashed" are no longer adequate responses from technology providers who are the platform for company decisions, transactions, and interactions. Modern

Unseen Liability

business continuity depends on the uninterrupted and accurate flow of information, the mission-critical lubricant for any increasing number of businesses. Users, both consumer and professional, are demanding technology providers be more "accountable" (a.k.a. liable) for the products they create and deliver. That's a huge responsibility for an industry that doesn't much like to contemplate its downside.

Status: When Google's popular email service, Gmail, went down for more than two hours, affecting more than 100 million customers worldwide, users did not shrug their shoulders and quietly bemoan the status of technology today. They complained—loudly. Message boards and online forums steamed with complaints. The message posted on Google's support page apologizing for the inconvenience did little to quell the complaints. By the next day, a resident of Galway, Ireland, had filed a lawsuit. Lucky for Google their business model did not create the same interruption for business functions and processes, though this is a path Google is on. As the company becomes more of a business technology platform, technology interruptions like these will become much greater business liabilities.

The Gmail malfunction impacted cyber users throughout the world, especially in Europe and India. Apparently, only users accessing the Web version of the email service were experiencing problems, with

POP (post office protocol) downloading and mobile access through iPhone and Google's own G1 working fine. With the movement of Google into more critical information services for business customers, are those customers prepared to experience an outage of their mission critical provider like Google? Is Google?

The new watchword in technology is not growth or speed or interoperability. It is accountability. Technology users, especially businesses, think their technology should work because essentially it *has* to work. When it doesn't, they're demanding redress.

Mandate: Technology providers must hedge against the unseen liabilities the technology industry has created for itself and for others. Like the inventor of a new pharmaceutical product, technology innovators must be prepared for the success stories as well as the negative side effects. In order to continue its creative process, the industry must hedge against the failures or unintended consequences that its wares have unleashed.

Education

Of the industries mentioned so far, education is the laggard in both technology adoption and in understanding its eventual risks. In many ways, universities are their own planets of norms, social networks, and opinions. The history of a cloistered culture made education professionals

Unseen Liability

less inclined to chase the latest technology or efficiency. But Web 2.0 changed that. The advent of social media broke through the walls around the education system and created a buzzing marketplace of ideas, commentary, rumors, gossip, and connection—all supported by university-owned technology. Riding the wave of a youthful takeover of Internet protocol and interaction, the unseen liability has arrived at the door of the educational institution. It is the Wild West of opinions and textual impulses playing out over the worldwide *college* web.

Exposure: During the first decade of the Internet (Web 1.0), education's primary exposure to technology risk was in the area of IP infringement and exposures related to professional publishing. As such, most universities transferred these exposures to media-professional liability insurance policies. When Netscape and other peer-to-peer sites emerged, students became big users of pirated entertainment, from movies to music. Their passion for their favorite bands was matched only by their outrage at being told ripping it off was not legal just because it was possible. In this venue, the primary role of the educational system was to educate. But the university could still operate at arm's length from technology abuses, errors, or ignorance.

In recent years, the role and impact of education technology changed dramatically as other technology risks emerged on campus.

Online universities, online college aid applications, and exploding social media sites for students placed universities in the bull's-eye of information malpractice. Ratings of professors, gossip about administrators, and rants about policy empowered students to take their social and professional lives online, for better or worse; often they invoked the name or the technology platform of the university itself. Professors blogging about students and students blogging about professors raised the stakes for claims of libel, slander, and defamation, not to mention misappropriation of ideas. The notion that such commentary enters into the world of public record has not soaked into the mind-set of most educators or the boards of those educators. As for the risks to personal reputations, it appears that students themselves underestimate the long tail of the Internet and the data hangover that may face them in the future.

  The trend in education is more personal data, more exchanges of opinion, and more lawsuits, all enabled by technology. As college students' profiles continue to grow as a very lucrative data demographic, personal information about them has become a hot asset in the black market of data brokers. As repositories (if not warehouses) for all manner of data about their students, colleges have become major targets of data thieves. In fact, during 2008, Privacy Rights Clearinghouse reported more than twenty-five data privacy breaches at American universities. Colleges store data about students' and their families' financial information,

Unseen Liability

performance information, and now even social information. Such a wealth of data may be necessary for colleges to operate at low cost and greater efficiency, but it also opens them up to new liabilities; they are no different than other data marts like Amazon, eBay, or Bank of America.

Status: Universities are already feeling the impact of data privacy breaches as a major exposure to their reputation and their bottom line. Again, UCLA offers an example. In 2006, hackers accessed the institution's system and the personal information of 800,000 students, alumni, staff, and even parents. Sensitive information stored in the database included Social Security numbers, home addresses, dates of birth, and contact information. UCLA was compelled to staff a call center to handle questions, set up a website with information, handle the negative media attention, and last but certainly not least, deal with the software flaw that allowed the hacker access in the first place.

On the social media front, colleges have been forced to contend with content issues far beyond IP infringement. When a Duke University student invented Juicycampus.com and invited students to post gossip, rumors, and rants related to colleges and universities in the United States, traffic was strong. And so was the backlash. Early advertising networks eventually backed away for fear of brand damage by association. Universities began to take disciplinary action against students who posted or were ousted for behaving badly on the site. CNN covered the growing concern among students that the un-moderated, anonymous nature of the site invited a new level of nastiness, rumor, and gossip. Individual campuses began to ban it. In February 2009, the initiative ran out of money and ceased operation, at least for now. Lawsuits, like the one from a University of Delaware student who says her reputation was damaged by the site, are still pending.

Mandate: Universities cannot be passive to the changing technology environment. They need it as much as any other industry. However, university leaders must recognize the shift in professional exposures and take up a more proactive role as technology monitors. They must understand the nature of what they allow and support via their networks and develop policies to protect the educational community and the institution itself from harm.

Conclusion: All businesses must confront the reality of technology risk and unseen liability. The issue is not one for future generations; the effects are already being felt. Data breaches are on the rise and so are their costs. According to a recent study by the Ponemon Institute:

Unseen Liability

- The cost of a data breach is rising. The average total cost per company was more than $6.6 million per breach in 2008, up from $6.3 million in 2007 and $4.7 million in 2006.

- When companies lose data, they also lose customers. Lost business accounts for 69 percent of breach costs, up from 65 percent in 2007, compared to 54 percent in the 2006.

- Organizations that have built their brand on trust have more to lose from a data breach. Trust may be intangible and hard to quantify, but the result of breaking that trust is clear. Consumers are prepared to walk if they believe their trust is misplaced and their data is at risk.

- The liability of privacy breaches is expected to rise significantly

The key to facing this new reality is a better understanding of technology-related risks and legal liabilities. IT is an asset, a weapon, and a blind spot for many industries that increasingly rely on data, software, networks, and the Internet.

There is no avoiding the issue: as technology has intertwined itself with business, risk has come along with it. The question now is not *whether* your business will face an unseen liability—be it a data breach or

IP infringement or reputation hit—but *when* will it occur. Considering the costs of legal uncertainties, technology liability insurance for business is likely to undergo a significant spurt of growth.

Unseen Liability

Chapter 9: Advertising 2.0—Building Our Own Mousetrap

History will see advertising as one of the real evil things of our time. It is stimulating people constantly to want things, want this, want that.

— Malcolm Muggeridge

One of the consequences of my specialty in technology is that when I use the Internet, I can often detect the wheels of the Internet economy turning, masking the hidden and increasingly complex transactions of data fields, cookies, crawlers, APIs, and content pop-ups. I know that *little*, if any, of what I experience in the way of online advertising is random or accidental. In fact, it's quite the opposite. I know that the proliferations of ads I see are not the result of traditional metrics of reach and frequency. The smart ads are mathematically, automatically, and precisely targeted at my eyeballs, engaging my "intent" with unparalleled and unprecedented precision. And I know that whatever I do, whatever I click on, every one of my key strokes may be collected, analyzed, sorted, and leveraged to figure out exactly what will make me open my wallet. If there is a universal "opt out" from today's Internet I have yet to discover it, let alone believe it possible.

The Internet advertising machine is like a sentient being. It is constantly learning, gathering, and interpreting data. It is always looking for new and better ways to get my attention, my intentions, my dollars, and my loyalty. I know, because I do this for a living, that I am participating in my own seduction as a consumer. With each keystroke, I am helping the Internet advertising world build a better mousetrap to catch me. I need the Internet, and the Internet is constantly building its intelligence of exactly what I need.

So far in our mass consumer use of the Internet, that level of understanding is not too widespread. But what if this user naïveté, this innocence, were to change as a result of the commercial abuses or professional neglect around personal data privacy? What would happen if millions of consumers around the globe figured out just how closely their Internet activities are monitored and how much of their personal data is at risk? What happens when the world's consumers and Internet surfers realize that the fabled Big Brother of the information age isn't the government, but a consortium of search and ad businesses, poised with unmatched power to separate us all from our money, or our sense of personal confidentiality and identity? Is the Internet ecosystem, the dominant environment of the information age, ready for the potential backlash of a privacy crisis and meltdown of our collective trust? What

Unseen Liability

happens if our faith in the Internet is torpedoed by an irresponsible or overly ambitious keeper of our data?

In this chapter I'll examine the cultural, legal, and commercial impacts of Advertising 2.0—the fierce melding of advertising and technology. I'll look at what has happened to the advertising industry in the Internet era, look at where unseen liability is lurking, and, finally, what needs to be done to protect the valuable public asset—*trust*—that has become the engine oil for ongoing consumer participation in the Internet.

Where we are now.

In many ways, the Internet saved the advertising industry. It gave it a new and more efficient platform, an entirely unchartered medium on which to create and sell advertising. It allowed advertising to achieve new efficiencies and make itself attractive to cost-conscious business clients. And in no small way, the Internet injected an element of newness and creativity into the advertising world. As with virtually every other American industry, the advent of new technology was good for advertising.

But all good things have a flip side. As was the case with other industries, the injection of Internet technology into the advertising industry created great new opportunities—and new liabilities with previously unconsidered consequences. Over the last decade the rapid introduction and advancement of information technology has continuously outstripped the traditional rules and regulations that govern most industries. As a result, classic print and media professionals in advertising found themselves having to operate in new fields of undiscovered experience that relied on websites, servers, and databases. The consumers who fed the new model of advertising were just along for the ride, and few of us even knew it. Whether we like it or not, ever since the Internet went mass market we have all been busy building our own, uniquely individual and personal cyber mousetraps. We are no longer persons; we are digital people comprised of a compilation of electronic attributes, tags, and fields within not just one database but a networked web of many.

What companies know about their customers has grown both deeper (they know more about us) and wider (they know it about more people). The average company, in fact, doubles its amount of stored data every year. Massive drops in data storage costs have fueled this drive for more, not less, data. With the rapid growth in personal data being collected and the increased capability of technology to act upon this information, ads are smarter, more targeted, and more entangled in every aspect of our personal business than ever before.

Ads on today's Internet are:

- More *targeted* based on who you say you are. A student? A mother? A Red Sox fan? If you've entered the information into any online site, forum, kiosk, or even typed it in a personal email message using a service such as Gmail, advertisers (I mean the machines) know.

- More *relevant* based on what you are doing. Are you considering a ski vacation? Job hunting? Looking for true love?

- More *personal* based on who your friends are. With whom do you Twitter? Who did you Friend? How do those networks link you to new people? What is your social graph of friends and connections?

- More *intelligent* based on where you are. In the office? At Starbucks? On the beach?

- More *intrusive* based on what you are writing or emailing or texting. Who else can read your email, and what are they doing with that data?

- More *deceptive* based on behavioral data and historical data. What links have you clicked? What networks have you joined by opening an email? How much privacy do you forfeit without really being aware of it?

The sheer volume of personal information advertisers now have access to is creating a new conversation around the very real possibilities of mass profiling, the automated engine of one-to-one marketing. What professional advertisers may deem "contextual advertising" or "cross-selling," others may view with more skepticism. What is the distinction between what advertisers are doing and surveillance? Depending on one's country and culture, what is universally *acceptable* with profile-based ads will vary greatly. I learned this personally when speaking at a Web 2.0 conference in Berlin in the fall of 2008. The German citizen's view of data aggregation and profile-based advertising was wildly different from the view held by attendees at a New York conference held a few weeks prior. It is the lack of legal and professional clarity of this advertising line and its newness that breed emerging blind spots for businesses, and therefore new claims related to possible advertising liability.

Marketing departments may argue that they are simply doing everything they can to get to know their customers better and provide them with the best and most targeted advertising possible. After all, who wants to waste time seeing ads for unwanted items? Wouldn't it be better to see only the ads relevant to our previously expressed interests? Are we willing to give up privacy for efficiency, and to what extent? If my

Unseen Liability

presentation in Berlin was any indication, this is the start of a debate that will impact not only the online advertising world but also the entire Internet economy. What do advertisers or marketing departments know? Should they know it? Who gave them permission, and for how long? What are they doing with that information? And how do consumers feel about it? This is the very fluid and rapidly changing intersection between technology and privacy that is already shaping the information age.

How we got here.

It's not as if advertising had been completely unregulated before the explosion of the Internet. Indeed, the industry has been closely supervised since the 1950s. The problem, as is the case for many industries, is that the regulations, case laws, and protections were crafted around an advertising industry that no longer exists. The industry that focused primarily on print, television, and radio—basing its decisions on formulas to secure the best reach and frequency—has largely been replaced. The regulations have not kept up with the techniques, capabilities, and unintended consequences of interactive advertising that touch individuals multiple times per day.

If you've ever watched the cable television drama *Mad Men*, you have taken a glimpse into the advertising world of the pre-Internet age. Long before the Internet, the US government passed laws protecting the privacy of consumers' personal information and shielding them from misleading, fraudulent, and deceptive advertising practices. The regulations crafted in and around that era focused on the intentions of the advertiser and the effect of the ad. The mantra was "truth in advertising."

The basic tenants were:

- Advertising must be truthful and not misleading (i.e., transparent).
- Advertisers must have evidence to back their claims (i.e., factual).
- Advertisements cannot be unfair (i.e., honest).

These were the guiding principles of the industry for decades. But the advent of new technology made the interpretation of concepts such as truth, fairness, and transparency more complicated. For example, is advertising based on a user's social behavior "fair," especially when a person may never realize their friends are fair game? Is search advertising based on anonymous user ratings "misleading?" Is sharing customer data to accelerate exposure on an ad network "truthful?" A gap between existing laws and expanding Advertising 2.0 practices began to emerge, along with the liabilities the gap created.

New Internet-era regulations come into being.

Unseen Liability

In an effort to provide more clarity around acceptable Advertising 2.0 practices, the Federal Trade Commission (FTC) recently expanded its standards of acceptability for advertising online.

For example, the guidelines called for more visible disclosures. Companies are now required to place disclosures on the same Web page as the claim they apply to and, when necessary, provide adequate visual cues to indicate that a consumer must scroll down on the page to view the disclosure.

The FTC also suggested more obvious hyperlinks. When hyper linking to disclosures, companies are required to make the link "obvious and noticeable" by labeling the link accurately and indicating its importance. Companies must place the link near relevant information, make certain the link takes consumers directly to the disclosure, and monitor link usage to ensure its effectiveness.

And the FTC had another guideline: no tricks. Ensure that an advertisement's text, graphics, hyperlinks, or sound do not distract consumers' attention from the disclosure. This is a wild card, in my view, to determine what is "distracting" and what is not. Herein lies yet another area of uncertainty to determine what you *can* do with advertising and what you *should* do. The FTC gave guidelines but not with great specificity.

The FTC has also recently made it clear that retailers are on the hook for online advertising that strays from "acceptable standards." If a company sells another firm's products, the FTC can hold that company responsible for misleading ads and product descriptions, even when those materials are provided by the manufacturer. The FTC and litigation attorneys specializing in cyber law pay close attention to online ads that make health or safety claims, or that present data or statistics consumers would have difficulty verifying. This creates new and heightened risks for health and lifestyle companies as they increasingly push the envelope on interactive ads that match a person's lifestyle, health, or social profile.

To compound the compliance risks of Advertising 2.0, federal lawmakers have jumped into the fray. The US Congress enacted several new laws that govern Internet advertising and privacy. The most important of these is HR 29, more commonly known as the SPY Act (Securely Protect Yourself Against Cyber Trespass Act), which went into effect on March 5, 2005. The act prohibits specific types of Internet advertisements and methods for manipulating users' computers, including:

- Advertisements that cannot be closed "without undue effort or knowledge by the user."

- Advertisements that can only be closed by "turning off the computer or closing all sessions of the Internet browser for the computer."

- Modifying a computer user's browser settings so that a different Web page appears when the browser is launched.

- Changing a computer user's default ISP (Internet service provider) as well as any settings associated with these connections.

- Altering a "list of bookmarks used by the computer to access Web pages."

- Altering any "security or other settings of the computer that protect information about the owner or authorized user for the purposes of causing damage or harm to the computer or owner or user."

- "Collecting personally identifiable information through the use of a keystroke logging function."

At least part of the reason for these new laws was to educate the vast army of new practitioners in the advertising space. Previously, the individuals who understood the power of technology were not the individuals schooled in the ethics of marketing, and vice versa. Although advertising was once its own, relatively isolated department of statisticians and creative writers, it was now substantially intertwined with information technology and privacy laws. Technologists were now were deploying, piloting, and understanding the latest advertising and personalization technologies. But they were doing so with a focus on technology, not on the potential consumer backlash. As a result, and surely without intent, the IT department had become an advertising liability.

Addressing Privacy

Never before have we imagined so much of our personal information in the hands of perfect strangers. Privacy has become linked forever with advertising, and as such new compliance risks are on the horizon. The SPY Act was passed during the Web 1.0 run up, in addition to several new state data privacy laws—forty-four in total! The laws and SPY Act addressed Internet consumer privacy issues, particularly the use of information collection programs installed on a user's computer to gather information about that user. The act defines an information collection program as one that collects personally identifiable information and either sends the information to anyone other than the computer user or uses the information to display advertising on that user's computer.

Before a company can install and execute such a program, the user must be given notice of the program's data collection functions and

Unseen Liability

consent to the program's execution. The act states that notice of the program's information collection functions must be clear, conspicuous, written in plain language, and clearly distinguished from any surrounding text or information. Further, the program must contain one of the following statements (or something substantially similar), depending on the program's exact function:

- "This program will collect and transmit information about you. Do you accept?"
- "This program will collect information about Web pages you access and will use that information to display advertising on your computer. Do you accept?"
- "This program will collect and transmit information about you and will collect information about Web pages you access and use that information to display advertising on your computer. Do you accept?"

The goal of such privacy laws is clear: bring the consumer into the process so that individuals can consent to the use of their information, not wonder if it's being lifted surreptitiously. With more than 120 million people already notified of a privacy breach incident, it is clear that personal data is a currency and a liability for doing business in the information age. The fact that these laws have been written supports the premise that privacy will be a legal, commercial, and cultural debate for years to come. As during other periods of commerce, this debate will lead to new arguments for liability, neglect, and malicious intent as they pertain to the highly personal world of Advertising 2.0.

The Coming Backlash

Even with recent regulation for advertising and privacy, a foreseeable gap exists between the practice of Advertising 2.0 and the acceptance of the consuming public. Companies enamored with the possibility of technology-infused advertising are continuing to innovate and turn their creations loose into the Internet economy. And they are finding more and more often that consumers are pushing back.

For example, in 2007 Facebook launched the program Beacon as part of its advertisement system. Beacon sent data from external websites to Facebook, for the purpose of facilitating targeted advertisements and allowing users to share their activities with their friends. Certain activities on partner sites—for example, what an individual purchased there—were to be published on the Facebook users' page for all that individual's Facebook "friends" to see. Consumer reaction was swift and negative. Although Facebook considered this new technology a great new innovation, consumers felt it invaded their privacy. Facebook officials were forced to spend time and money altering their advertising initiative to conform to public tastes and apologizing for misunderstanding their consumers' preferences in the first place. Beacon has become a prime example of the gap between technologists and consumers. Technologists live in the bubble, where technological innovation can only be good. Consumers are not always in agreement.

In another example, this one from 2008, Sears launched a community portal called managememyhome.com. The goal was to provide an online space where Sears shoppers could download product manuals, find product tips, and get home renovation ideas. The website had a feature called "Find your products" designed to help users look up past purchases. The project was a clear effort to promote the Sears brand via the growing popularity of online communities. But the technology of the advertising effort outpaced the protections. In short order, a security firm discovered a flaw in the portal that allowed Sears customer purchasing history to be available online. Sears disabled the "Find your products" feature, but the damage was done. The company faced a class action lawsuit and a black eye as a user of Advertising 2.0 tactics.

The debate continues. When it became clear that Google was planning to use its AdWords contextual advertising technology to scan users' email and deliver ads based on the email content, consumer reaction was negative and online blogs were filled with voices of dissent. The initiative is still under debate; the professional standard of care has yet to be written.

Not all efforts are missteps or professional blind spots. Wal-Mart, for example, has made a change to its online advertising whereby it increases the transparency of online ad delivery. Consumers can see online ads and click on a link to get an explanation as to why that ad was delivered. By pulling back the virtual curtain and exposing some of the mystery behind online advertising, Wal-Mart has created a greater sense of consumer trust, potentially lowering its advertising liability risk in the process.

In many instances, companies came out with a technology-inspired advertising or marketing tactic, sure it would be a big hit, only to be surprised by the backlash from consumers. Clearly, the gap between what technology can do in the advertising space and what consumers consider acceptable still exists.

What can be done to mitigate the risks?

Managing and anticipating the liability of Advertising 2.0 can be addressed on several fronts.

Building Community and Awareness: The advertising industry and traditional companies that use online advertising need to fully and

Unseen Liability

continuously discuss the evolving standards of care as they relate to protecting personal data, advertising with transparency, and identifying the "bad actors" within their industry. As data-fed advertising expands and leverages all the latest technological platforms—such as social network advertising, search advertising, mobile advertising, and behavioral advertising—companies that want to use these techniques must also be willing to talk to – *and listen to* - consumers about their experiences, concerns, fears, and opinions. To not do so would be to advertise at their own peril, and do not assume your IT department is giving the subject much consideration.

It is increasingly essential for practitioners of Advertising 2.0 technologies to step outside their bubble and hear what users have to say about the innovations. The mission of marketers to achieve one-to-one marketing must be balanced with the mission of consumers to retain their privacy and control of their personal data. The happy medium between business and consumer interests can only be found if professionals take the time to listen, observe (with permission!), and contemplate any potential abuses or neglect of the system. As is the case in any other area of business or politics, excess and abuses of professional power create very real and costly liabilities.

Controls and Governance: The risk mitigation controls around the advertising industry can surely be updated to meet the new technological risks. The new controls must ensure transparency and at a minimum attempt to support the guidelines set forth by FTC, state, and professional industry guidelines. Positions like chief privacy officer or chief security officer are examples of new roles that seek to keep organizations in good standing with the power and potential scrutiny of the technology-powered business.

These controls may also take the form of government regulation, industry standards, or legal precedent. But any laws for the world of cyber liability and Advertising 2.0 must be developed in concert with the professionals they are attempting to govern. And they must be clearly communicated so that a common standard of care can be established for the information age. In parallel with the creation of controls, there must be a greater emphasis on training and compliance so that the innovators of new advertising technologies understand the legal, ethical, and societal norms governing their efforts. They are the architects and engineers of the digital future, and as such they need to develop a sense of professional integrity to make their trade a sustainable and admired craft.

Protections through Risk Transfer: Even with the most professional practitioners and well-understood standards of care,

Unseen Liability

accidents, abuses, and neglect will still occur. The virtual worlds of online advertising and the Internet economy will be no exceptions. The online advertising industry can acknowledge the unseen liabilities and uncertainties that new technologies have created. By doing so, they take the first step toward considering risk transfer concepts, like insurance, to help give themselves a more predictable, if not sustainable future. This is the newest profession that must look for ways insurance can hedge against risk.

Ultimately, these types of steps must be taken to deal with emerging blind spots, not just to protect consumers and advertisers, but to protect the overall Internet environment. If issues and potential abuses regarding consumer privacy and online ad transparency are not addressed, consumers may come to the conclusion that their information is not safe or respected in the online world. This customer pullback would be a crisis in trust that no one in the Internet industry would benefit from. A universal and massively executed "opt out" by millions of Internet users would stall many of the wonderful benefits recent technology provides. If consumers withdraw their participation and if companies leave themselves uninsured for catastrophic blind spots, the economic engine of the Internet will surely falter—for all of us.

Chapter 10: The Organizational Impact of Technology Risk

Technology is a way of organizing the universe so that man doesn't have to experience it.

- Max Frisch

This book thus far has focused on the threats and business uncertainties raised by new technology and business's broadening use of the Internet. I've argued that the business insurance solutions we have today focus far too heavily on errors made by human beings and not enough on expanding hazards created by new technology. This chapter backs up a moment and revisits that thought. Because although it's true that unseen liability is created by the new technology, I don't mean to suggest that human error is a thing of the past…far from it.

This chapter will look more closely at the human factors of unseen liabilities. Many aspects of managing human capital have been changed by the use of new technology: hiring, training, managing, and firing. Most assumptions for effective management of employees have been reconfigured by the advent of the Internet, again by Web 2.0, and will be again by the new technologies coming down the pike. Meanwhile, few human resources (HR) departments have kept pace. Indeed, they are often the last to know how technology-enabled employees have created new corporate blind spots.

Technology has created new areas of unseen liability for both the human resources department and the process of managing employees throughout the workforce. In fact, no department has been untouched by the impact of employee empowerment through technology. For HR in particular, here are some potential ways to mitigate employee-manifested blind spots.

Be proficient at cyber-sleuthing. The process of recruiting and hiring has become increasingly virtual, and that has left many tried and true methods of vetting candidates in the dust. In the pre-Internet days, HR would be covered if it verified the data on a resume and called all the listed references. Today, technology has created many new areas of information that HR must investigate. Does the individual in question have a website? A MySpace site? A history of blogging or participation in online forums? If so, is this information relevant to the job he or she is seeking? Could the company potentially be embarrassed—or even at risk legally—if the individual's cyber life were to be publicly discussed? The department responsible for the process of hiring now has a much broader field of data to collect on any one person. What HR does not know could come back to haunt the company.

Unseen Liability

Be proficient at virtual communication. Pre-Internet HR departments communicated by telephone, or even snail mail. A job offer or job rejection might conceivably arrive via the good old US Postal Service. Today, virtual communication is the norm and certainly the HR department must be able to react with the dexterity and speed the workforce demands. That's not as easy as it looks, even for the most cutting-edge companies.

In 2009, an employee in Twitter's HR department meant to tell 186 applicants for a posted product manager position that they were not being considered and sorry, better luck next time. But instead of using BCC (blind carbon copy) to hide applicants' identities from each other, Twitter HR goofed and sent them all the message using a standard carbon copy, which allowed each person to see who the other 185 applicants were. The slip up was widely reported in technology blogs, and Twitter CEO Evan Williams felt compelled to send the 186 an apology. Oops. Time, effort, and a sliver of Twitter's reputation for technology savvy fell victim to technology risk. Perhaps it was fortunate that a more negative outcome was not produced for one of the applicants, creating a claim against Twitter for information malpractice.

Be able to train others. HR is often where companies implement and manage their employee training functions. But training of new employees now means more than handing out parking passes and explaining the benefits packages. What are the rules and regulations surrounding the use of company technology? How are employees expected to behave online while at work? Or while traveling? Or on their own time? If employees can publish online with speed and no cost, what are the expectations for them to not create new liabilities for the company through their actions? HR must be able to articulate these expectations to new and existing employees.

An area of liability in which HR is often involved is termination. When an employee is let go, HR may be called upon to show that the move was justified or not discriminatory. If an employee is fired for not having proper technology skills, will the HR department be able to show tech skills were clearly part of the job description? Or that the employee was trained in these skills? Or evaluated for them?

Be able to handle the "rogue" employee. Perhaps the greatest challenge to HR in the Internet age is the individual no one ever sees coming. This is the rogue. It may be the nefarious character the name conjures up: the disgruntled employee who wants to "get" his boss, the angry lifer passed over for promotion, the laid-off help-desk staffer who still has access to working passwords. These are individuals who can wreak havoc on a company as revenge for perceived mistreatment. Rogue employees who

Unseen Liability

steal personally identifiable or company confidential data have created enormous liabilities for businesses that depend on data integrity and security. I'll argue, though, that the concept of a rogue employee must be more broadly applied than just privacy risk. Certainly, these intentional disruptors of IT qualify. But an employee can mean well and still be a rogue without knowing he or she is creating a new risk.

Consider, for example, the industrious employee blogging on his free time about all the interesting things he's heard around the office. Perhaps he has knowledge of a new product in the works or an executive about to leave or a lawsuit soon to be settled. Or maybe he repeats negative comments overheard about his company's competition. His casual release of these material events—even well meaning, in an effort to boost the company's reputation—can backfire. This loyal employee is also a rogue. He is a technology-enabled unseen liability, loose on the Internet. He is an HR headache, no matter how well intentioned he may be.

In addition to mastering these new skills, HR and risk managers must look to how they deal with other departments.

The IT Department

Once a satellite department, much like HR itself, IT has emerged as *the* mission-critical function when it comes to business continuity and mitigating liability. The IT infrastructure for larger companies has moved to the central core of the company, and all other departments revolve around it. Few business tasks remain in the modern company that do not involve the activities of IT. Technology has become the thread that runs throughout a company, joining departments and binding their success, and their failure, together.

A risk manager's role in supporting the IT department needs to be to help technologists understand the downside and liabilities of their increasingly critical functions. If for years IT was its own universe, then today it must be integrated into the whole analysis of enterprise risk, with deeper evaluation of what liabilities and disruptions can be created because of technology failures or technology abuses. This integration may take a variety of forms. HR, risk professionals, and business managers charged with supervising IT efforts must communicate not just the goals of the technology, but the risks of technology to the organization. IT must begin to see not only what it does for the organization but what it could do *to* the organization. IT must understand the economics of failure, not just as they relate to itself, but to the company as a whole and even to the greater marketplace of the Internet community. If this mind-set does not spring from within, it must be managed into the department. Most important, technologists should also become more knowledgeable about risk transfer solutions that go beyond technology alone. The notion

Unseen Liability

of technology risk insurance should be as valued by IT personnel as it is by risk managers.

<u>Marketing</u>

This is yet another department transformed by the technology revolution and involved in information age risks the company may never have imagined. Armed with new technology tools, marketing can reach out to customers in novel and more targeted ways. Yes, even down to what was once the Holy Grail: one-to-one marketing. Sales and marketing can also collect more personal data on customers and use that information to create even more successful marketing programs.

Technology-enabled marketers should consider the unseen liability of this new marketing machine as well as its positive possibilities. How is the data being guarded? What data is being collected and why? How well is the company communicating with its customers about the data it collects? Does the company understand the different laws of data collection and storage across different countries? Contextual marketing and personalization in one country is "surveillance" in another.

These are the emerging concepts that can be lost in the excitement of doing something new and different. Risk managers must be trained to be the proverbial wet blanket of the marketing department. Sure, it sounds great. How can it go wrong? Are we prepared if that eventuality happens? And are we insured if we overstep the legal boundaries of technology self-governance?

A good example of this new mandate in action would be a viral campaign. It may sound great to marketing: cheap, fast, impactful, and broad. What's not to like? The question then becomes how well trained and managed the marketing staff is to evaluate not only the pros, but the cons of this campaign. Are marketing staffers educated by their managers and by company policy to understand rules and regulations surrounding technology use? Do they know the legal definition of spam? Can they tell you whose email they can use and why? Is this campaign consistent with the company's terms of use? Do these email addresses have the protection required by industry and government standards? It's not enough for the marketing department to come up with great new uses for technology. It must also be smart about what's legal, appropriate, and acceptable in customers' eyes. If that's not bubbling up from the rank and file of the marketing experts, then it must be taught by managers and those in the highest levels of the company.

Senior Executives

The role and responsibility of senior managers in technology issues has shifted. No longer is it reasonable for this upper layer of management to take a hands-off approach to a company's technology risks. Stock prices can drop, financials destroyed, and reputations torpedoed by large-scale technology blunders. The C-suite of the information age must evolve.

New Senior Roles: A variety of new senior management titles are necessary as companies move forward to address the issues of technology risk. Does a company have a chief privacy officer? What about a chief security officer? Soon we will see data asset officers. These are critical roles for any firm that cares about its technology-based risks and rewards. Firms without these positions will be considered ill equipped to compete and poorly prepared to mitigate against technology risks and liabilities.

New Oversight: Technology can no longer be left to the occasional check-in. As the vital core of all operations, senior management must consistently and actively monitor it. That means knowing what's going on inside the department as well as what is transpiring out in the world. What are the new regulations brewing in Washington? What are the latest cultural norms surrounding technology? Senior management must be willing to be plugged in to technology both inside and outside the walls of the firm. It is not a side topic for experts to ponder, but a central issue to every move the firm will make. Consider this: business has increasingly moved to more self-service models in a quest for lower costs, improved productivity, and better customer service.

This means that technology error now trumps human error when considering the liabilities of the future company and professional organization.

New Valuations: What are the company's true assets? As we move forward in an information economy, what is the role of brick and mortar versus data bits? How are both valued? How are they protected? What gains and risks does each bring to the table? How is the company set to cope with that reality? As guardians of shareholder value, senior management and boards must appreciate their role in this process and how technology has changed it.

Finally, HR must be able to keep its own house in order. Like a bank, human resources departments were once rooms that held file cabinets full of personal information. Today, they are computers and servers and clouds into which massive amounts of highly sensitive employee information is funneled. This information is of great value to the company; it is indicative of its salary structure, its hiring and firing trends, its benefits and investments. This information is also highly prized by the individuals who work for the firm. It will be evidence of their performance reviews, their salary history, their reprimands or honors.

All this information is considered valuable. HR will have the mandate to collect and protect it. Just like the database of a bank or

Unseen Liability

retailer, the database of a company has information that can be considered a valuable asset. Is HR trained to protect it? Is the company insured for it? And if not, whose job it is to see that information is safeguarded?

In the landscape of unseen liability, it's important to remember that no matter how many machines and programs take over our day-to-day tasks, the impact of human beings on the process is still significant. The managing of people is still a job for people. How well those managers are prepared to navigate the new pitfalls of technology may be unknown. But the need for people trained in those jobs could not be clearer. The information worker is here to stay. Insuring for the errors, impulses, and intentions of information workers is a new risk management imperative.

Unseen Liability

Epilogue: Post Web 1.0—Our Lives among the Clouds

The most exciting breakthrough of the 21st century will not occur because of technology but because of an expanding concept of what it means to be human.

- John Naisbitt

During the first generation of the Internet (1995–2005), retroactively referred to as Web 1.0, companies had their first taste of interactive marketing in their online pursuit of what they termed one-to-one marketing. The premise of one-to-one was simple. With a newly achievable (and affordable) database of very basic user profiles, a large company could begin to market and sell its products and services to customers in a more personalized, relevant way. By matching profile elements of select users with similarly matched content and products, the company could offer the user a more engaging experience with the expectation that they would spend more time, money, or both on the site. New parents were pitched baby products. College students got entertainment information. Aging boomers saw pharmaceutical ads. As with many technology initiatives during the first Internet wave, business momentum grew quickly to implement personalized e-commerce and informational websites. The rush was on to eliminate guesswork from the marketing and advertising industry.

Personalization was the buzz. Everyone wanted to be the Amazon.com of their industry. "Really get to know your customer!" was the hot business mantra. One-to-one technologies like BroadVision and newly minted e-commerce sites emerged and were embraced as the enablers to make personalization a reality, right down to the personalized home pages for news, commerce, and marketing interactions. As a society, this was our first step down the path of personalized, interactive marketing with no way, or desire, to turn back. The dawn's early light of the information age was barely and irreversibly upon us as consumers, customers, parents, and citizens.

Did we get what we expected?

As with most business imperatives that spread too wide too quickly, there were reasonable successes and overhyped failures. Blue-chip companies like American Airlines, Home Depot, and Wal-Mart all found significant value in online personalization, but no organization quite reached the holy grail of a true and consistent one-to-one relationship with its customers. Simply put, users were more conservative with their personal data, and the companies showed restraint and caution in even asking for it.

Unseen Liability

Through 2001, the movement of one-to-one everything began to reach its natural limits. After the tragedy of 9/11, economic growth slowed and the business fever for personalization cooled dramatically. By 2002, those businesses, consultants, and users that participated in Web 1.0 with its vision of one-to-one marketing were left scratching their heads with the looming question of "what happened?"

In hindsight, one-to-one marketing was so popular during Web 1.0 largely because the business premise was so obvious and seemed so achievable: use online interactions to help a company know its customers better, learn from their behavior, and anticipate their needs with more targeted ads, content, and offers. It was an alluring business promise in the glow of Internet newness, and for several years the industry made some meaningful strides. Web 1.0 did in fact get better. But when the bottom fell out in 2001, especially for corporate e-business initiatives, the pursuit of one-to-ne marketing was chilled and left for another day, a new CIO, a better technology, and a more data-sharing universe of Internet users. But technology did not hold still and wait for better times. Technology, like time itself, moves on.

Web 2.0: Adolescence

If Web 1.0 was about the first iteration of interactive marketing, then the effort could be summed up as serving company-approved content and ads to registered users with nascent user profiles. Companies dabbled and Internet users experimented. In hindsight, Web 1.0 was all quite new and idealistic, if not innocent. A website could float the occasional "cookie" in an attempt to establish very basic user relevancy, but very few companies at that time could create data warehouses of deeply identifiable, rich profiles without the users actively adding personal attributes to their own profile. "Tell us more" prompts encouraging users to share more personal data were common carrots from clumsy websites that would gladly reward data-sharing customers with slightly broader site access or basic newsletter services. This exchange of personal data for site rewards, home pages, etc. was the first indicator that personal data was in fact becoming a *valued currency*, even if most businesses still could not act upon it.

Web 1.0 and the pursuit of one-to-ne marketing still had the semblance of user control and e-business transparency. Within these new e-commerce "relationships" trust was surprisingly good, yielding a market-driven balance between users' personal data judgment and businesses' advertising restraint. Then Web 2.0 came along and that balance within the ecosystem was harder to strike.

A Fundamental Shift

Unseen Liability

As an industry and as a society we have gone from our Internet childhood, full of data innocence and permission-based advertising, to our Internet adolescence, awash in personal data over sharing and advertising overindulgence. Today's Web 2.0 environment appears to lack concern for what we leave in our digital wake, a mutual indictment of voracious, data-fed advertisers and overly bold users. In many ways, Web 2.0 is not a perfect progression of Web 1.0 aspirations. For example, social Web users appear too willing to give up something of value (their highly personal attributes of social, commerce, and professional dimensions) for what feels right at the moment, but with little apparent consideration their privacy and reputation exposures down the road.

The concept of one-to-ne marketing was executed (albeit not to completion) under the mutual expectation that a user would share their profile with a company for better products and services, and the company would honor its intimacy and confidentiality with the user. One-to-one marketing was a major technology-enabled advancement that appeared to be practiced with prevailing business ethics for privacy respect and advertising restraint. Words like "data transparency," "privacy," and "identity controls" still made their way into coding decisions and advertising techniques. Put more simply, the company still considered the data of the user the *property of the user and not the property of the company*.

Personal data was parked securely in the company server, not surrendered to the Internet for eternity. Today, this distinction is significant.

A worrying transition has occurred over the last few years as Web 2.0—the hungrier, more ad-driven Web—has taken hold. People appear infinitely more willing to put it all out there about who they are, and companies are far too eager to make money from it. The result is billions spent annually for online advertising and database technologies. Web 2.0 has become a gold rush of personal data mining. It reaps windfall gains for those companies that can quickly collect it, package it, and sell it—and windfall losses of personal privacy for those users who too quickly give it up.

A Slippery Slope with Users Losing Control

If it continues on its current path, Web 2.0 may result in one-to-one marketing gone wrong. Indications are that personal data exchange is no longer the trusted interaction between modest users and restrained companies. No, the new mantra (albeit a secret one) is "one to one to many." Users may give the data once and have no control over were it goes from there. Resold and often stolen personal data has created almost infinite personalization possibilities for companies that acquire such detailed personal data, regardless of whether the weary Internet user wants to drop out of the system. Online ad networks are a new

Unseen Liability

phenomenon resulting from the demand and volume of personal data. In fact, the precision for messaging and advertising has never been greater. But again, with great power comes equally great responsibility.

Modern business now bears the burden of unprecedented personal data protection, a result of the massive data ownership shift from users who too readily share their personal information to the data zealous companies that collect it, package it, and make money on it. And what becomes of personalization as a result of this shift? Well, Web 2.0 could be personalization on steroids, and that's not a compliment. What is increasingly known and stored about individual users as consumers, workers, friends, parents, patients, and citizens has become the business of big business. This environment has created a targeting nirvana for advertisers and a challenge for privacy advocates and regulators.

One-to-one marketing was never meant to, in this my mind, cross the treacherous waters of personal privacy where knowing one's customer can reach almost perverted proportions. The direction of this trend and of the Web itself are of special concern, given the awe-inspiring amount of social data new users are willing to share . . . I mean surrender.

The Big Shift to a Data-Driven and Technology-Dependant Organizations

Over the last decade, economists and analysts have recognized that most traditional companies were organized and managed for a marketplace that no longer exists. Managing scarcity and control in the industrial age has been replaced by managing abundance and access in the information age. As we look beyond 2010, we can easily predict that the roles of information technology and the Internet will be even more pervasive, more mission critical, and thus riskier. Data and technology will drive and enable almost everything we do, from services to manufacturing. IT will organizationally and metaphorically move quickly to the center, the hub, the brain, and the concentration of risk.

During the first generation of the Internet, most businesses and professional enterprises still saw technology as a foreign plant, a marvel more than a mandate. Information professionals and their infrastructure of information technology were peripheral, supportive, and another layer of organizational cost and expense. Today, that orbit has been reconfigured. We have seen a dramatic shift over the last few years. Ever-increasing computing capability, network availability, and data economics have moved data infrastructures not just to a central role, but to a mission-critical one. It used to be said that "nothing happens until someone sells something." Today it can be said that "nothing happens until information does something."

Unseen Liability

This central importance and dependence on technology to work correctly has resulted in a greatly increased concentration of risk for most small and large businesses. Conducting an ever-increasing amount of transactions via the Internet and cloud servers has also caused us to consider the risks of unintended consequences and systemic exposures of interdependence. This book has been largely about alerting business and technology leaders to these risks, to what I have referred to all along as the unseen liability of the technology revolution.

The shift in organizational thinking, therefore, is a logical transition to (1) making money/creating wealth and (2) managing risks/hedging liabilities in the information age. The more provocative question at this point is where might risks of the information age go next? Although I am no scholar, prophet, or fortuneteller, I do feel compelled to offer a few directional predictions. This is my outlook for what is likely to happen—not sometime in the next generation, but in the foreseeable future of public, business, and legal affairs. It's the next iteration of my thesis, and it is under way as we speak.

Economic Predictions:

1. Business will continue to collect, store, and utilize unprecedented volumes of data.

2. The value of personal data, company confidential information, and digital electronic property will continue to grow.

3. Valuations of companies' performance will depend more precisely on their information assets and the valuations of their IT infrastructure and competencies.

4. The cost of technology-related risks and liabilities will grow in the areas of (1) data privacy expense and liability, (2) Internet liability for media and intellectual property, and (3) professional liability for errors resulting from technology failure.

5. Unseen liabilities will become more expensive for companies that poorly manage the landscape of Web 2.0, cloud computing, Internet and network security.

6. Capital will continue to move into technologies and companies that can harness an increasingly deep vault of information assets via a broad network of Internet properties.

7. The cost of using technology will go down while the costs of misusing technology will rise dramatically.

8.

Unseen Liability

The following are the technology developments likely to compound the risks and extend the uncertainties:

1. Cloud computing will create larger concentrations of risk related to privacy, IT governance, business continuity, and international regulation.

2. The economics of cloud computing will shift from the analysis of "cost to use" to the risk quantification of "cost to fail." This analysis will then drive greater financial backing of clouding structures; i.e., "cloud insurance."

3. The course of systemic risks for the Internet will depend upon balancing the economic gains of cloud computing against the catastrophic loss potential of technology failure, negligence, and abuse.

4. Search companies and ad networks will become massive data warehouses of highly personal, and eventually company, data assets.

5. Contextual everything: ad capabilities based on who, what, and where you are will outpace the ability of business to self-regulate, creating new liabilities for breaking laws yet to be written.

6. The social Web will dominate marketing, advertising, and marketing intelligence. Users will continue to

engage companies directly and indirectly via the participative Web, heightening the need for companies to monetize their place on the Internet and effectively manage against the unseen liabilities that online users and employees will create.

A cultural evolution on Internet awareness will catch some businesses by surprise:

1. Users, consumers, and subscribers to the Web 2.0 ecosystem will (1) be more cautious about their privacy and reputation, (2) become more unforgiving of technology errors by companies, and (3) will demand more transparency of how their data is being used, by whom, when, where, and why.

2. Liabilities for business will increase for companies that do not adequately anticipate changes in user expectations and attitudes as they relate to how companies engage them and protect their information.

3. CIOs will think more like IT economists and not just technologists; they will likely hedge IT uncertainties by transferring risk to insurance.

4. Reputation management will become a consideration and mandate for a broader number of Internet users.

Unseen Liability

Cyber insurance will grow in demand, breadth, and coverage:

1. Business insurance related to technology risks and liabilities will grow rapidly across traditional industries now depending on data infrastructures as their epicenter.

2. Cyber insurance will become more dynamic and effective in matching the speed of developments in technology.

3. Government will play a broader role in technology law, governance, and regulation; it will potentially require companies to insure for cyber disasters as a financial hedge to a more systemic risk to national economic security.

4. The price and availability of cyber insurance for unseen liabilities will likely grow, until such time that a more mature market exists to competitively price risks and liabilities of the information age.

Most if not all of these trends are currently under way. There is no reason to believe we are anywhere near the end of our technology revolution. We can bet on the fact that there will be a Web 3.0, something beyond cloud computing, and more beyond that. We can believe that the users of technology and the Internet—both businesses and consumers—

will want more speed, more efficiency, and more connectivity but also more security and predictability. And we can expect the innovators of the field to stand and deliver while bad actors are more easily identified and penalized for polluting the Internet environment.

How will business adapt to the opportunities and risks of the information age? If the last fifteen years is any indication, we will see windfall gains for companies that maximize their information assets and windfall losses for companies that mismanage information risks and underestimate their information liabilities.

Information technology and the open Internet have opened many doors. But they will remain open only as long as a critical mass of Internet users *trust* and *participate* in the digital ecosystem. Leaders of companies will further realize that technology creates enormous blinds spots and unintended consequences. If ignored, these blind spots are a threat to both business predictability and the public good of the Internet itself. Web 2.0 could be the globe's brightest hour or dumbest blunder, should the world's user community decide en masse that commercial or governmental use of technology has gone too far and the major enterprises of technology progress have lost control, restraint, and the security of personal data.

Unseen Liability

Technology is an enriching yet demanding partner in the modern business world. Professional mastery in the use of technology—*respect* for it, in fact—can offer any business the real potential for growth, innovation, and success. Emerging laws and customer-driven demands will require that the risks of technology be understood, managed, and when appropriate, insured. Understanding unseen liabilities is the mandate *now*, in 2010, for any business or professional organization seeking sustained success in the information age.

The benefits of information technology and the open Internet will almost always outweigh the risks, uncertainties, and unintended consequences of our collective blind spots, as long as business leaders firmly address the unseen liabilities in their midst. As I stated at the outset, today's global problems are solved with information, while future problems will be caused by information abuses, negligence, and ignorance. With the health, sustainability, and *security* of the world's virtual environment at stake, this is one subject that should be of interest to us all.

2018 and Beyond

Although this book was originally released in 2010, as is, it took the world this long to realize that the intersection with technology was not only an economic disruption but a cultural and social change that will alter the world norms as we know them. Where we go from here just might make us ponder much larger concerns, whether recent advances in artificial intelligence, data science and cyber risks require a new framework for truly considering Information Age values and ethics altogether.

At the current pace of technology advances, what is "technical" may no longer be the matter by 2020, but rather what is "tech-thical," what is right and wrong, in a society predicated and altered irreversibly by technology. Information ethics and the evolution of information malpractice likely becomes the next frontier of laws, business, culture and conflicts. And that book will soon write itself…

Unseen Liability

Author Biography

Drew Bartkiewicz is a businessman, inventor, author and serial entrepreneur. He is best known as the Founder and CEO of mobile communications company, lettrs, and is the patent inventor of mobilizing cyber signatures, "SignID." Mr. Bartkiewicz has been involved with the World Economic Forum's Future of the Internet initiative since 2009 and in 2016 was named a Top 100 Most Intriguing Entrepreneurs by Goldman Sachs. His company, lettrs, was named a Forbes Top 25 Veteran Founded Business that same year.

After managing the Southern Europe of salesforce.com, Mr. Bartkiewicz had founded cyber risk trading platform, CloudInsure, the first platform ever to leverage data analytics and financial instruments to hedge growing cyber risks. He has over 20 years of information technology experience and is a decorated combat veteran of the 82nd Airborne, having earned the Bronze Star medal in Iraq in 1991. He speaks four languages and is a graduate of the US Military Academy at West Point and the Yale University School of Management. He also published the first book of letters from a mobile network, "Poetguese," with Paulo Coelho, author of a worldwide best seller, "The Alchemist."

Drew Bartkiewicz resides in New York City and Connecticut with his wife, Araceli, and their three children Blake, Dane, and Ana.

www.ingramcontent.com/pod-product-compliance
Lightning Source LLC
Chambersburg PA
CBHW052247220526
45471CB00001B/228